KAREN BLIXEN
(Isak Dineser

AF202319

OUT OF AFRICA

Edited by: E. S. Odland
Illustrations by: E. S. Odland

The vocabulary is based on
Michael West: A General Service List of
English Words, revised & enlarged edition 1953
Pacemaker Core Vocabulary, 1975
Salling/Hvid: English-Danish Basic Dictionary, 1970
J. A. van Ek: The Threshold Level for Modern Language
Learning in Schools, 1976

Series editors: Ulla Malmmose
and Charlotte Bistrup

Consultant: Maggie Fortescue

Cover photo: Kilimanjaro,
Amboseli National Park by
CAR/2. maj

© EASY READERS, Copenhagen
- a subsidiary of Lindhardt og Ringhof Forlag A/S,
an Egmont company.
ISBN Denmark 978-87-23-90191-0
www.easyreaders.eu
The CEFR levels stated on the back of the book
are approximate levels.

Easy Readers

EGMONT

Printed in Denmark

KAREN BLIXEN
(1885-1962)

In **Out of Africa** Karen Blixen tells the absorbing story of her life in Kenya. It is a story of a woman's struggle to create a new existence on foreign soil. Her encounter with African culture changes her outlook on life.

With warmth and humanity these accounts illustrate her genuine affection for the African people, their dignity and traditions.

Karen Blixen was born in Rungsted, Denmark, in 1885. After studying art in Copenhagen, Paris and Rome, she married her cousin, Baron Bror von Blixen-Finecke, in 1914. Together they went to Kenya where they farmed coffee outside Nairobi. After their divorce in 1921, Karen Blixen continued to manage the coffee plantation until 1931 when a collapse in the coffee market forced her back to Denmark.

In 1934 she published **Seven Gothic Tales**, written in English under her pen-name Isak Dinesen. **Out of Africa** (1937) is an autobiographical account of the years she spent in Kenya. Most of her subsequent books were published in English and Danish simultaneously, including **Winter's Tales** (1942) and **The Angelic Avengers** (1946), under the name of Pierre Andrézel. Among her other collections of stories are **Last Tales** (1957), **Anecdotes of Destiny** (1958), **Shadows on the Grass** (1960) and **Ehrengard** (1963). **The Immortal Story** was filmed in 1968 by Orson Welles. Meryl Streep portrayed Karen Blixen in the film "Out of Africa" (1984), based on the books **Out of Africa**, **Shadows on the Grass** and **Letters from Africa** by Karen Blixen, **Isak Dinesen: the Life of Karen Blixen** by Judith Thurman and **Silence Will Speak** by Errol Trzebinski.

Baroness Blixen died in Rungsted in 1962.

1. KAMANTE

The Ngong Farm

cloud

I had a farm in Africa, at the foot of the Ngong Hills.
The Equator runs across these highlands, a hundred
miles to the north, and the farm lay over six thousand
feet above sea level. In the daytime you felt that you
5 were high up; near to the sun, but the early mornings
were clear and restful, and the nights were cold.

The *landscape* had not its like in all the world. There
was no fat on it and no rich growth of plants anywhere.
The colours were dry and burnt. The view was wide.
10 Everything that you saw made for greatness and free-
dom.

The chief feature of the landscape and of your life in
it, was the air. You breathed easily. Looking back on a
period spent in the African highlands, you get the
15 strong feeling of having lived for a time up in the air.
The sky was rarely more than a *pale* blue or *violet* with
many ever-changing *clouds* sailing on it, but it had a

landscape, all the features of an area of land that can be seen when
looking across it
pale, without much colour
violet, blue mixed with a little red

4

blue energy in it, and at a short distance it coloured the hills and the woods a fresh deep blue. In the middle of the day the air was alive over the land, it waved and shone like running water, doubled all objects, and created great *Fata Morgana*. In the highlands you woke up in the morning and thought: Here I am, where I ought to be. 5

The Mountain of Ngong *stretches* in a long range from north to south with four *peaks* like *immovable* blue waves against the sky. It rises eight thousand feet above the sea, and to the east two thousand feet above the country around it; but to the west the drop is deeper – the hill falls straight down towards the Great Rift Valley. 10

The wind in the highlands blows *steadily* from the north- north-east. It is the same wind that, down on the coasts of Africa and Arabia, they name the Monsoon, the East Wind, which was King Solomon's favourite horse. It runs straight against the Ngong Hills. The clouds, which were travelling with the wind, struck the side of the hill and hung round it, or were caught on the top and broke into rain. But those that took a higher course sailed clear of it and disappeared to the west, over the burning *desert* of Rift Valley. 15 20

From the Ngong Hills you have a unique view, you

Fata Morgana, an image of something which is not really there, caused by hot air conditions
stretch, extend; draw out
peak, the pointed top of a mountain
immovable, that does not move
steady, not changing
desert, a large area of land that has very little water and very few plants growing on it

5

see to the south the vast *plains* of the great *game* country that stretches all the way to Kilimanjaro; to the east
and north the park-like country of the foothills with
the forest behind them, and the hilly land of the
Kikuyu* *Reserve*, which extends to Mount Kenya a
hundred miles away – a pattern of little square *maize*-
fields, banana-*groves* and grassland, with here and there
the blue smoke from a *native* village. But towards the
west, deep down, lies the dry moon-like landscape of
the African low country, a brown desert with *bushes*
spread over it and riverbeds lined with dark green trees.

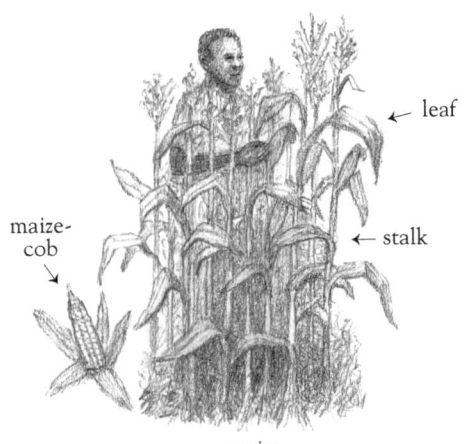

leaf

maize-
cob

stalk

maize

plain, a large area of flat land
game, wild animals or birds hunted for sport or food
*a people *native* to Kenya
reserve, an area of land set apart for a special purpose
grove, a group of trees; a small wood
native, belonging to a place by birth, production or growth; one that is
born, or that which is grown, in a particular place
bush, a thickly branched, low-growing plant; also, in Africa, an area of
wild land covered with trees and bushes

We grew coffee on my farm. The land was a litte too high for coffee, and it was hard work to keep it going; we were never rich on the farm. But a coffee-*plantation* is a thing that gets hold of you and does not let you go, and there is always something to do on it: you are gen- 5 erally just a little behind with your work.

Coffee-growing is a long project. It does not all turn out as you imagine when you are young and hopeful. First you carry the boxes of your shining young coffee-plants to the field in the streaming rain, and watch all 10 the farm-hands set the plants in regular rows in the wet ground. Then you do all you can to protect them from the sun, with branches broken from the bush. It will take four or five years before the trees bear fruit. In the meantime you will get *drought* or diseases. Some of the 15 trees have been badly planted and will die just as they begin to flower. You plant a little over six hundred trees to the *acre*, and I had six hundred acres of land with coffee; my *oxen* slowly drew the *cultivators* up and down the fields, between the rows of trees, many thousand 20 miles.

There are times of great beauty on a coffee-farm. When the plantation flowered at the beginning of the rains, it was a bright sight, like a white cloud in the *mist* and the *drizzling* rain, over six hundred acres of land. 25

plantation, a large farm where coffee, tea, sugar, or the like, are grown
drought, a long period with no rain
acre, a measure of land, about 4050 square metres
ox/oxen, see picture, page 9
cultivator, a tool (or machine) used for cultivating the soil, that is
breaking it up and preparing it for growing plants
mist, a cloud of tiny drops of water hanging just above the ground
drizzle, to rain lightly, with many fine drops

7

When the field turned red with the *ripe berries*, all the
women and children, whom they call the **totos**, were
called out to pick the coffee off the trees, together with
the men. Then the *wagons* and *carts* brought it down to
5   the factory near the river. Our machinery was never
quite what it should have been, but we had planned
and built the factory ourselves and thought highly of
it. Once the whole factory burned down and had to be
built up again. The big coffee-dryer turned and turned,
10 and sometimes the coffee would be dry and ready to
take out of the dryer in the middle of the night. That
was a moment of special beauty, with many *hurricane
lamps* in the huge dark room of the factory, and *eager*

ripe, (of fruit) ready to be picked
berry, here, the fruit of the coffee plant, inside which is the coffee
bean, from which coffee is made
wagon, *cart*, vehicles with two and four wheels, pulled by horses or
oxen
eager, full of interest

8

ox

shining dark faces, in the light of the lamps, round the dryer. Later on the coffee was sorted by hand and packed in *sacks*.

Then in the end, in the early morning, while it was still dark and I was lying in bed, I heard the wagons *loaded* with coffee-sacks, twelve to a ton, with sixteen oxen to each wagon, starting on their way into Nairobi railway station up the long factory hill, with much noise, the drivers running beside the wagons. I was

hurricane lamp

sack

load, anything that is being carried, especially something heavy; to put a load in or on something or somebody

9

pleased to think that this was the only hill up on their way, for the farm was a thousand feet higher than the town of Nairobi.

In the evening I walked out to meet them coming
5 back, the tired drivers and oxen with hanging heads in front of the empty wagons, with a tired little toto leading them. Now we had done what we could. The coffee would be on the sea in a day or two, and we could only hope for good luck at the big *auction-sales* in Lon-
10 don.

I had six thousand acres of land, and had thus got much *spare* land besides the coffee-plantation. Part of the farm was native forest, and about one thousand acres were squatters' land, what they called their
15 **shambas**. The squatters are Natives, who with their families hold a few acres on a white man's farm, and in return have to work for him a certain number of days in the year. My squatters, I think, saw the relationship in a different light, for many of them were born on the
20 farm, and their fathers before them, and they very likely regarded me as a sort of superior squatter on their estates.

Each Kikuyu family had a number of small round peaked *huts*; the space between the huts was a lively
25 place; here the *goats* were milked, and children and chickens were running about.

I had, moreover, a couple of thousand acres of grassland on the farm. Here the long grass ran like sea waves

---

auction-sale, a public event at which things are sold to the person who offers the most money for them
spare, extra; more than needed or used

10

before the strong wind, and the little Kikuyu *herd*boys herded their fathers' *cows*.

Nairobi was our town, twelve miles away, down on a flat bit of land amongst hills. Here was the Government House and the big central offices; the country 5 was ruled from here.

When I first came to Africa, there were no cars in the country, and we rode in to Nairobi, or drove in a cart with six *mules* to it. Here you could buy things, hear news, lunch or dine at the hotels and dance at the 10

herd, a group of cows or oxen; to look after such a group
mule, an animal that is the young of a horse and a *donkey*, which is an animal of the horse family with short legs and long ears

Club. And it was a lively place, in movement like running water, and in growth like a young thing, it
changed from year to year, and while you were away on
a shooting safari.

5   The Swahili* town, on the road to the Muthaiga
Club, had not a good name in any way, but was a lively, dirty and colourful place.

The Somali** town was farther away from Nairobi,
on account, I think, of the Somali system of *seclusion*
10 of their women. It lay open to all winds, it must have
made the Somali think of their native deserts. The
women had *dignified*, gentle ways, and were *hospitable*
and *gay*, with a laughter like silver bells. I was much at
home in the Somali village through my *servant* Farah
15 Aden, who was with me all the time that I was in
Africa, and I went to many of their *feasts*.

The Somali were *cattle*-dealers and traders all over
the country. They bring much trouble upon themselves
by their terrible *tribal quarrels*. Farah belonged to the
20 *tribe* of Habr Yunis, so that in a quarrel I sided with

*a Bantu people on the east coast of Africa and Zanzibar, influenced
by Arab and Persian culture; today also the official Bantu language in
Kenya and Tanzania
** a member of an East-Hamitic race (like the ancient Egyptian or the
modern Berber), partly of Arab, Negro, and other origin
seclusion, the state of being (kept) apart from others
dignified, having *dignity*, that is a calm and serious manner
hospitable, pleased to welcome guests
gay, happy and full of fun
servant, a person who works in a private house for wages
feast, a large meal, especially in honour of some event, like a wedding
cattle, cows and oxen are cattle
tribal, of a *tribe*, a group of people of the same race, sharing the same
language, religion, etc
quarrel, an angry argument

them. At one time there was a big fight in the Somali town, between the two tribes of Dulba Hantis and Habr Chaolo, with shooting and fires, and ten or twelve people killed, before the Government took action.

Before I took over the management of the farm, I had 5 been out on many safaris. But when I became a farmer I put away my *rifles*.

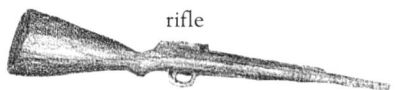
rifle

The Masai*, the *nomadic*, cattle-owning people, were neighbours of the farm and lived on the other side of the river. From time to time some of them would 10 come to my house to tell me about a lion that was taking their cows, and to ask me to go and shoot it for them, and I did so if I could. I also walked out on the Orungi plains to shoot a zebra or two as meat for my farm labourers, with many optimistic young Kikuyu fol- 15 lowing me. I shot those birds on the farm that were good to eat. But for many years I was not out on any shooting safari.

From my first week in Africa, I had felt a great *affection* for the Natives. The discovery of the dark races made 20 my whole world larger and richer. If someone with an

*members of an African people living in the highlands of Kenya and Tanganyika
nomad, a member of a tribe or people that moves with its animals from place to place
affection, a warm gentle feeling of caring for or loving somebody

13

ear for music had happened to hear music for the first time when he was already grown up, his case might have been similar to mine. After I had met with the Natives, I set out the routine of my daily life to the orchestra.

It was not easy to get to know the Natives. They were quick of hearing and quickly disappeared from sight. If you *frightened* them they could *withdraw* into a world of their own, in a second, like the wild animals which at a sudden movement from you are gone – simply not there. Until you knew a Native well, it was almost impossible to get a *straight* answer from him. To a direct question as to how many cows he had, he would reply – "As many as I told you yesterday." It goes against the feelings of Europeans to be answered in such a manner, it very likely goes against the feelings of the Natives to be questioned in this way. If we pressed them, to get an explanation out of them, they moved backwards as far as they possibly could and tried to lead us on the wrong track.

We could not know, and could not imagine, what the dangers were that they feared from our hand. Or in the end their behaviour to us might be some sort of strange *joke*, and the *shy* people were not afraid of us at all. The Natives have far less the sense of risks in life than white people. Perhaps they are, in life itself, within their own element, such as we can never be. This

---

frighten, to make afraid
withdraw, here, to go back or away from a place, an event, etc, or from other people
straight, here, direct
joke, a thing said to make people smile or laugh
shy, afraid or unwilling to speak in the presence of others

confidence they had, I thought, because they had *preserved* a knowledge that has been lost to us; Africa will teach it to you: that God and the *Devil* are one, the *majesty co-eternal.*

On our safaris, and on the farm, my *acquaintance* with 5 the Natives developed into a settled and personal friendship. We were good friends. I got used to the fact that while I would never quite know or understand them, they knew me through and through. When the Natives felt safe with us, they would speak to us a great 10 deal more openly than one European speaks to another.

At times, life on the farm was very lonely, and in the quiet of the evenings life seemed to be *seeping* out of you, just for lack of white people to talk to. But all the time I felt the silent existence of the Natives running 15 parallel with my own, on a different level.

A Native Child

Kamante was a small Kikuyu boy, the son of one of my squatters. I used to know my squatter children well, for they worked for me on the farm, and used to be up round my house herding their goats on the *lawns,* in the 20 hope that here something of interest might occur. But

preserve, to keep something in its original state
Devil, the greatest evil being
majesty, king
co-, together
eternal, that lasts forever
acquaintance, personal knowledge, gained through contact; a person whom one knows but who is not a close friend
seep, to flow very slowly
lawn, an area of short grass in a garden

15

Kamante must have lived on the farm some years before I ever met him; I suppose that he had been leading a lonely existence like a sick animal.

I came upon him for the first time one day when I 5 was riding across the plain of the farm, and he was herding his people's goats there. He was the most *pitiful* object that you could set eyes on. His head was big and his body terribly small and thin and both his legs were covered with deep, running *sores*. When I stopped and 10 spoke to him, he did not answer, and hardly appeared to see me. His eyes were like those of a dead person. He looked as if he could not have more than a few weeks to live, and you expected to see the *vultures*, which are never far away from death on the plain, high up in the 15 pale burning air over his head. I told him to come round to my house the next morning, so that I could try to *cure* him.

I was a doctor to the people on the farm most mornings from nine to ten, and like all great *quacks* I had a 20 large circle of patients, and generally between two and a dozen sick people waiting outside my house.

The Kikuyu are *accustomed* to the unexpected. Here they are different from white men, of whom the majority try very hard to *insure* themselves against the

pitiful, causing one to feel *pity*, that is to be very sad about the troubles and sufferings of others
sore, a painful place on the body where the skin is injured
vulture, a large bird that eats the flesh of dead animals
cure, to make somebody healthy again
quack, a person who claims to have special knowledge and skill, especially in medicine, without having it
accustom oneself to something, to make oneself familiar with something or accept something as normal or usual
insure, to take measures to protect oneself against loss or harm

unknown and the *assaults* of *fate*. The Africans are on
friendly terms with *destiny*, having been in her hands
all their time. They face any change in life with great
calm. Amongst the qualities they will be looking for in
a master or a doctor or in God, imagination, I believe, 5
comes high up on the list. That is why I was popular
and famous as a doctor.

When I first came out to Africa I travelled on the
boat with a great German scientist, who was going out,
for the twenty-third time, to experiment with cures for 10
sleeping-sickness. He told me that his difficulty with
the native patients had never been any lack of *courage*
in them – in the face of pain or of a great operation they
generally showed litte fear – but it was their deep *dislike*
of anything regular, of any repeated treatment, that the 15
great German doctor could not understand. But when I
myself got to know the Natives, this quality in them
was one of the things I liked best. I sometimes thought
that what, at the bottom of their hearts, they feared
from us was *pedantry*. In the hands of a *pedant* they 20
would die of *grief*.

I knew very little of doctoring, just what you learn
on a first aid course. But I had become famous as a doctor because of a few chance lucky cures, and the big
mistakes that I had made had not changed that. 25

assault, attack
fate, the power believed to control all events and against which one
cannot do anything; what will happen or has happened to somebody
destiny, fate
courage, the ability to face fear, pain, opposition, etc
dislike, a feeling of not liking somebody or something
pedantry, too much concern about formal rules or small details
pedant, person with such a concern
grief, a feeling of being extremely sad

If I had been able to cure all my patients, who knows but that their circle might have thinned out? Would they still have been sure that the Lord was with me? For the Lord they knew from the great years of drought,
5 from the lions on the plains at night, and the *swarms* of *grasshoppers* that would come on to the land, nobody knew where from, and leave not a *leaf* of grass where they had passed. They knew him, too, from the unbelievable hours of happiness when the swarm passed
10 over the maizefield and did not settle, or when in spring the rains would come early and make all the fields and plains flower. So that this highly capable German doctor might be after all a sort of *outsider* where the real great things in life were concerned.

grasshopper

15 To my surprise Kamante turned up at my house the morning after our first meeting. He stood there, a little away from the three or four other sick people present, *erect*, with his half-dead face, as if he had now made up his mind to try this last chance of holding on to life.
20 He showed himself with time to be an excellent patient. He came when he was ordered to come and he

swarm, a large number of birds or *grasshoppers*, flying together
leaf, see picture, page 6
outsider, a person who is not, or is not accepted as, a member of a society, group, etc.
erect, in an upright position

18

could keep account of time when he was told to come back every third or fourth day, which is an unusual thing with the Natives. He bore the hard treatment of his sores without showing any signs of pain.

Rarely, rarely, have I met such a wild creature, a human being who was so completely *isolated* from the world, so closed to all surrounding life. He had no wish for any sort of contact with the world around him, and no pity for the tears of the other sick children, when they were washed and *bandaged*, but he never looked at them either. It seemed that nothing could be so bad as

bandage →

| *isolated*, having little contact with other people

to surprise him: he was prepared for the worst. All this was in a *grand* manner, but in a person of his size it was an attitude to make you lose heart.

As far as my doctoring of him went, things did not, however, look hopeful. For a long time I kept on washing and bandaging his legs, but the disease was beyond me. From time to time he would grow a little better, and then the sores would break out in new places. In the end I made up my mind to take him to the hospital of the Scottish *Mission*.

I had the Church of Scotland Mission as my neighbour twelve miles to the north-west, five hundred feet higher than the farm; and the French Roman Catholic Mission ten miles to the east, on the flatter land, and five hundred feet lower. I did not *sympathize* with the missions, but I was on friendly terms with them both, and felt sad that between themselves they should live in a state of *hostility*.

The French Fathers were my best friends. I used to ride over with Farah, to hear Mass with them on Sunday morning, partly in order to speak French again, and partly because it was a lovely ride to the mission.

It was an extraordinary thing to see how the Church of Rome carried her atmosphere with her wher-ever she went. The Fathers had planned and built their church themselves. It was a fine big grey church with a bell-tower on it; it was laid out around a broad courtyard, in

---

grand, dignified; excellent; large
mission, a group of religious people sent out to teach others about the Christian faith, here to Africa; a building or group of buildings where this work is done
sympathize, to be in agreement with
hostility, the state of not agreeing to the point of being enemies

the midst of their coffee-plantation, which was the oldest in the *colony* and very well run.

The friendly fathers offered me a glass of wine after
mass and during the conversation they would draw any
sort of news out of you that you might possibly have. 5
But while they were so interested in the life of the
colony, they were all the time in their own French way
exiles. If it had not been for the unknown, higher
authority that kept them in the place, you felt they
would not be there. For when they were called back, all 10
of these would leave the affairs of the colony to themselves and go straight back to Paris.

The Scottish Mission I did not know so well. There
was a *splendid* view, from up there, over all the surrounding Kikuyu country, but all the same the mission 15
gave me an impression of being blind, as if it could see
nothing itself. The Church of Scotland was working
hard to put the Natives into European clothes, which,
I thought, did them no good from any point of view.
But they had a very good hospital at the mission. They 20
saved the lives of many of the people from the farm.

They kept Kamante at the Scottish Mission for three
months. He came back to my house on the morning of
Easter Sunday, and handed me a letter from the hospital people who declared that he was much better and 25
that they thought him cured for good. He must have
known something of its contents, for he watched my

colony, a group of people who have settled in a foreign country but
subject to control by the parent country
exile, a person who lives away from her or his country from choice or
because forced to do so
splendid, grand; excellent; very beautiful

face with interest while I was reading it, but he did not want to discuss it, he had greater things on his mind. Kamante always carried himself with much dignity, but this time he shone with *triumph* as well.

5 Kamante had carefully tied old bandages round his legs, to arrange a surprise for me. It was clear that he saw the great importance of the moment, not in his own good luck, but, not thinking of himself, in the pleasure that he was to give me. He probably remem-
10 bered the times when he had seen me all upset by the failure of my cures with him, and he knew that the result of the hospital's treatment was a wonderful surprise. As slowly, slowly he removed the bandages there appeared a pair of whole *smooth* legs, only slightly
15 marked by grey *scars*.

When Kamante, in his calm grand manner, had enjoyed my great surprise and pleasure, he stated that he was now a Christian. "I am like you," he said. He added that he thought I might give him a rupee*
20 because Christ had risen on this same day.

He went away to call on his own people who lived a long way away on the farm. From what I heard from his mother later he told her of the *impressions* of strange people and ways that he had received at the Hospital.
25 But after this visit he came back to my house as if he took it for granted that now he belonged there. He was then in my service from this time until I left the country – for about twelve years.

triumph, the state of feeling very satisfied or pleased as the result of success or victory
smooth, having an even surface
scar, mark left on the skin after a sore has healed (become healthy)
*a unit of money
impression, an effect produced on the mind or feelings of somebody

When I first met Kamante, he looked as if he were six years old, but he had a brother who looked about eight, and both brothers agreed that Kamante was the elder of them, so I suppose he must have been set back in growth by his long illness; he was probably then 5 nine years old. He grew now, but he was always very short, and his legs remained forever very thin. He had in him something bright and alive; in a painting he would have made a spot of unusually strong colouring. He was never quite right in his head, or at least he was 10 always what, in a white person, you would have called highly *eccentric*. He was all his life, in his own way, an isolated figure. Even when he did the same things as other people he would do them in a different way.

I had an evening school for the people of the farm 15 with a Native schoolmaster to teach them. I got my schoolmasters from one of the missions, and in my time I have had all three – Roman Catholic, Church of England, and Church of Scotland schoolmasters. My school was to me a favourite place on the farm, the 20 centre of our *spiritual* life, and I spent many pleasant evening hours in the long old store-house in which it was held.

Kamante would then come with me, but he would not join the children, he would stand a little away from 25 them, as if closing his ears to the learning. But alone in my kitchen, I have seen him copying from memory, very slowly, those same letters and figures that he had observed on the blackboard in the school.

---

eccentric, not conventional or normal; slightly odd
spiritual, of the human spirit and soul

He had a little *mocking* laugh, of which he made use in all circumstances, but chiefly towards any self-confidence in other people. It gives all Natives a great pleasure when things go wrong, which in itself is hurt-
5 ful and extremely unpleasant to Europeans. Kamante brought this characteristic to a rare *perfection*, even to a special self-*irony*, that made him take pleasure in his own *disappointments* and *disasters*, nearly exactly as in those of other people.

10 Kamante began his life in my house as a dog-toto; later he became a medical assistant to me. There I found out what good hands he had, although you would not have thought so from the look of them, and I sent him into the kitchen to be a cook's boy under my old cook Esa,
15 who was murdered. After Esa's death he succeeded him, and he was now my *chef* all the time that he was with me.

Natives have usually very little feeling for animals, but Kamante was different here, as in other things. He
20 was a very good dog-boy, and he identified himself with the dogs, and would come and tell me what they wished, or missed, or generally thought of things. He

mock, to laugh at or make fun of something or someone in an unkind way
perfection, the state of being perfect
irony, the expression of one's meaning by saying the direct opposite of what one is thinking but using tone of voice to indicate one's real meaning
disappointment, the state of being sad or not pleased because one or someone has failed or some desired event has not happened
disaster, a very bad accident that causes great damage or loss of life
chef, (French), a professional cook, especially a chief cook in a restaurant

24

kept the dogs free of *fleas*, and many times, in the middle of the night, he and I, called by the *howls* of the dogs, have, by the light of the hurricane-lamp, picked off them, one by one, the terrible big *ants*, the **Siafu**, which eat up everything on their way.

flea ant

He must also have used his eyes at the time when he had been in the mission hospital, because he was a good doctor's assistant. After he had left this office, he would at times appear from the kitchen to give me very good advice in case of sickness.

But as a chef he was a totally different being. It was something you cannot explain, as ever where you are dealing with *genius*. If Kamante had been born in Europe, and had fallen into the hands of a *clever* teacher, he might have become famous. Out here in Africa he made a name for himself, his attitude to his art was that of a master.

I was much interested in *cookery* myself, and on my first visit back to Europe, I took lessons from a French chef at a famous restaurant, because I thought it would

howl, the long, loud cry of a dog; to make such a sound
genius, an unusually great mental ability or ability to create a work of art
clever, showing intelligence or skill; quick at understanding and learning
cookery, the skill and practice of cooking

25

be a pleasant thing to be able to make good food in Africa. Now when I found Kamante at hand, as a familiar spirit to cook with, this interest again took hold of me. Kamante, in all cooking matters, was sur-
5 prisingly clever with his hands. The great *tricks* of the kitchen were child's play to his dark hands. They knew on their own everything about omelettes, vol-au-vent*, sauces, and mayonnaises. He had a special gift of making things light. He disliked all *complicated* tools, and
10 when I gave him a machine for beating eggs, he set it aside and beat whites of eggs with a *weeding* knife that I had used to weed the lawn with, and his whites of eggs towered up like light clouds.

He had a great memory for *recipes*. He could not read
15 and he knew no English, so that cookery books were of no use to him. He named the dishes after some event which had taken place on the day they had been shown to him, and spoke of the sauce of the grey horse that died. There was only one thing he refused to learn: that
20 was the order of the courses within the meal. So it became necessary for me, when I had guests for dinner, to draw pictures for my chef. I didn't quite believe that this was because he could not remember, but he did, I think, in his own heart, maintain that there is a limit
25 to everything and that upon anything so completely unimportant, he would not waste his time.

---

trick, here, the best way of doing something; a particular technique
*a light round open "cake" (made without sugar), filled with a mixture of meat, fish or other food, usually served with a sauce
complicated, not simple
weeds are the wild plants that are growing where they are not wanted. To weed is to remove them.
recipe, a set of instructions on how to prepare a food dish

It was a moving thing to work with him. In the course of our co-operation, I felt not only the kitchen, but the whole world in which we were co-operating, pass over into Kamante's hands. For here he understood to perfection what I wished of him, and sometimes he carried out my wishes even before I had told him of them.

Kamante could have no idea as to how a dish of ours ought to taste. He was, in spite of his connection with civilization, at heart a Kikuyu and had faith in the traditions of his tribe as the only true way of living. He did at times taste the food that he cooked, but he made strange faces and stuck to the maize*cobs* of his fathers.

I sent Kamante to the Muthaiga Club to learn, and to the cooks of my friends in Nairobi, when I had had a new good dish in their house. By the time he had learned all they could teach him, my own house became famous in the colony for its table. This was a great pleasure to me and I was glad when my friends came out to dine with me. Kamante remembered the individual taste of those of my friends who came most often to the farm. "I shall cook the fish in white wine for Bwana* Berkeley Cole," he said *gravely* as if he were speaking of a mad person. "He sends you out white wine himself to cook fish in."

One night, after midnight, he suddenly walked into my bedroom with a hurricane lamp in his hand, silent, as if on duty. It must have been only a short time after

maize-*cob*, see picture, page 6
*master, boss; a term applied by natives in Africa to a European
grave, serious and important; giving cause for worry

27

he first came into my house, for he was very small. He spoke to me very gravely. "Msabu*," he said, "I think you had better get up." I sat up in bed surprised; I thought that if anything serious had happened, it would
5 have been Farah who would have come to *fetch* me, but when I told Kamante to go away again, he did not move. "Msabu," he said again, "I think that you had better get up. I think that God is coming." When I heard this, I did get up, and asked him why he thought
10 so. He gravely led me into the dining-room which looked west, towards the hills. From the door-windows I now saw a strange sight. There was a big grass-fire up in the hills and the grass was burning all the way from the hilltop to the plain. It did indeed look as if some
15 huge figure was moving and coming towards us. I stood for some time looking at it, with Kamante watching by my side. Then I began to explain the fire to him. I meant to calm him, for I thought that he had been terribly frightened. But the explanation did not seem to
20 make much impression on him one way or the other. "Well, yes," he said, "it may be so. But I thought that you had better get up in case it was God coming."

---

*a native term of respect for a European lady
fetch, to go and find and bring back someone or something

The *Savage* in the *Immigrant's* House

One year the long rains failed.

That is a terrible, *tremendous* experience, and the farmer who has lived through it will never forget it. Years afterwards, away from Africa, in the wet climate of a northern country, he will start up at night, at the sound of a sudden *shower* of rain, and cry, "At last, at last."

In normal years the long rains began in the last week of March and went on into the middle of June. Up to the time of the rains, the world grew hotter and drier every day.

The Masai, who were my neighbours on the other side of the river, at that time set fire to the dry plains to get new green grass for their cattle with the first rain, and the air over the plains danced with the powerful fire and clouds of grey smoke rolled along over the grass, and the heat and the smell of burning were carried along over the cultivated land.

When the quickly growing sound moved over your head it was the wind in the tall forest trees – and not the rain. When it ran along the ground it was the wind in the long grass – and not the rain. When it *rustled* just above the ground it was the wind in the maize fields – where it sounded so much like rain that you were taken in, time after time – and not the rain.

savage, wild; violent. Here the savage is Old Knudsen
immigrant, a person who has come to live permanently in a foreign country
tremendous, very great in size, amount, power or effect
shower, a short period of rain or snow
rustle, to make a dry light sound like paper or leaves

But when the earth answered like a *sounding-board* in a deep *fertile roar*, and the world sang round you, all above and below – that was the rain.

But one year the long rains failed. It was, then, as if the Universe were turning away from you. Everything became drier and harder, and it was as if all force and beauty had withdrawn from the world. It was not bad weather or good weather, but an absence of all weather. All colours *faded*; the smells left the fields and forests.

With every day, in which we now waited for the rain *in vain*, prospects and hopes of the farm grew smaller, and disappeared. All the work of the last months turned out to be labour of fools. The farm work slowed down, and stood still.

The Natives became silent during the drought. It was their existence which was at risk; it was not an unheard-of thing to them – and had not been to their fathers – to lose nine-tenths of their stock in the great years of drought. Their shambas were dry, with a few *withering* sweet potato and maize plants.

After a time I learned their ways from them, and gave up talking of the hard times. I was young and I had to collect my energy on something, if I were not to be blown away with the dust on the farm-roads, or the smoke on the plain. I began in the evenings to write

---

sounding-board, a thin plate of wood in a musical instrument increasing sound
fertile, producing or bearing fruit
roar, a deep long cry like that of a lion; a loud cry of pain, anger or laughter
fade, to lose colour
in vain, without success
wither, (of plants) to dry up and die

30

stories that would take my mind a long way off, to other countries and times.

I had been telling some of the stories to a friend when he came to stay on the farm.

At first I only wrote in the evenings, but later on I often sat down to write in the mornings as well, when I ought to have been out on the farm. It was difficult, out there, to decide whether we ought to remove the withering coffee berries from the trees to save the trees, or not. I put the decision off from day to day.

I used to sit and write in the dining-room, with papers spread all over the dinner table, for I had accounts of the farm to do, in between my stories, and sad little notes from my farming manager to answer. My houseboys asked me what I was doing; when I told them I was trying to write a book, they looked upon it as a last attempt to save the farm through the hard times, and took an interest in it. They would come in and stand for a long time watching the progress of it, keeping me company with their backs to the wall.

Kamante sometimes stood by the wall for an hour in the evening. One night he said, "Msabu, do you believe yourself that you can write a book?"

I answered that I did not know.

To figure to oneself a conversation with Kamante one must imagine a long pause before each *phrase*. All Natives are masters in the art of the pause and thereby give perspective to a discussion.

Kamante now made such a long pause, and then said, "I do not believe it."

I had nobody else to discuss my book with; I laid

| *phrase*, a group of related words

down my paper and asked him why not. I now found that he had been thinking the conversation over before, and prepared himself for it; he stood with the Odyssey* itself behind his back, and now he laid it on
5 the table.

"Look, Msabu," he said, "this is a good book. It hangs together from the one end to the other. Even if you hold it up and shake it strongly, it does not come to pieces. The man who has written it is very clever.
10 But what you write," he went on, "is some here and some there. When the people forget to close the door it blows about, even down on the floor and you are angry. It will not be a good book."

I explained to him that in Europe the people would
15 be able to fix it all up together.

"Will the book then be as heavy as this?" Kamante asked.

"No," I said, "it will not, but there are other books in the library, as you know, that are lighter."

20 "And as hard?" he asked.

I said it was expensive to make a book so hard.

He stood for some time in silence by the table and waited, and then asked me gravely: "Msabu, what is there in books?"

25 As an example, I told him the story of Odysseus and Polyphemus, and how Odysseus had called himself Noman, had put out Polyphemus' eye, and had escaped tied up under a *ram*.

Kamante listened with interest and expressed as his
30 opinion that the ram must have been of the same race

*the story of Odysseus, as told by Homer in the 8th century BC
ram, an adult male sheep

32

as the sheep of Mr Long, of Elmentaita, which he had seen at the cattle-show in Nairobi. He came back to Polyphemus, and asked me if he had been black, like the Kikuyu. When I said no, he wanted to know if Odysseus had been of my own tribe or family.   5

"How did he," he asked, "say the word, **Noman**, in his own language? Say it."

"He said **Outis***," I told him. "He called himself Outis, which in his language means Noman."

"Must you write about the same thing?" he asked   10
me.

"No," I said, "people can write about anything they like. I might write about you."

Kamante who had opened up in the course of the talk, here suddenly closed again; he looked down at his   15
body and asked me in a low voice, what part of him I would write about.

"I might write about the time when you were ill and were out with the sheep on the plain," I said, "what did you think of then?"   20

His eyes moved over the room, up and down; in the end he said: "**Sejui**" – I know not.

"Were you afraid?" I asked him.

After a pause, "Yes," he said, firmly, "all the boys on the plain are afraid sometimes."   25

"Of what were you afraid?" I said.

Kamante stood silent for a little while, then he looked at me; his face became deep, his eyes looked *inward*:

*Greek for nobody
inward, into the mind or soul

"Of Outis," he said. "The boys on the plain are afraid of Outis."

A few days later, I heard Kamante explain to the other houseboys that in Europe the book which I was
5 writing could be made to stick together, and that with terrible expense it could even be made as hard as the Odyssey, which he showed them. He himself, however, did not believe that it could be made blue.

He often referred to himself as a Christian. I did not
10 know what that meant to him, and when I asked him he then explained that he believed what I believed, and that, since I myself must know what I believed, there was no sense in questioning him. He had put himself under the God of the white people. In his ser-
15 vice he was prepared to carry out any order, but he would not take upon himself to give reasons for a working system which might prove to be as unreasonable as the working systems of the white people themselves.

It sometimes happened that my behaviour did not
20 agree with the teachings of the Scottish Mission, where he had been *converted*; then he would ask me who was right. The respect for the Christian religion in Africa was *weakened* by the *intolerance* that one Christian church showed towards the other.
25 On Christmas eve, while I was in Africa, I used to drive over to the French Mission to hear Midnight Mass. It was generally hot at this time of the year; as you drove through the plantation, you heard the mis-

convert, to change one's religion
weaken, to make or become weak or weaker
intolerance, the state of not being willing to accept ideas, opinions or behaviour different from one's own

34

sion bell a long way in the clear warm air. A crowd of happy, lively people were at the square round the church when you arrived, the French and Italian shop-keepers of Nairobi with their families had come out, and the Natives wore colourful clothes. The big fine church was lit with many hundred *candles*. 5

When Christmas came, in the first year after Kamante had come into my house, I told him that I was going to take him with me to the Mass, as a fellow Christian, and described to him the beautiful things 10 that he was going to see there. Kamante listened to it all, moved in his soul, and put on the best clothes he had. But when the cart was at the door, he came back with a troubled mind and said that he could not possibly come with me. He did not want to give his reasons, 15 and would not answer my questions; in the end it came out. No, he could not go, he had by now realized that it was to the French Mission that I meant to take him, and he had so strongly been warned against that mission when he had been in hospital. I explained to him 20 that this was all a *misunderstanding*, and that he must come now. But at that he began to turn to stone before my eyes; he died, he turned up his eyes so that only the white showed in them.

"No, no, Msabu," he *whispered*, "I am not coming 25 with you. There inside that big church, I know it well, there is a Msabu who is **mbaia sana**," – terribly bad.

When I heard this I became very sad, but I thought

---

candle, see picture, page 36
misunderstanding, failure to understand something correctly or in the right way
whisper, to say something so quietly that only the people closest to one can hear

that now I would indeed have to take him with me so that the Virgin* herself could *enlighten* him. The Fathers had a life-size *statue* of the Virgin in their church, all blue and white, and the Natives are generally *impressed* by statues. So I promised Kamante my protection and took him with me, and when he walked into the church, very close behind me, he forgot all his worries. It happened to be the finest Christmas Mass that they had ever had at the mission. There was in the church a very big *Nativity*, just arrived from Paris, with the Holy Family. It had above it a blue sky with shining stars and round it a hundred *toy* animals, which must have given the Kikuyu tremendous pleasure.

← candle

nativity

*Mary, the mother of Jesus
enlighten, to give somebody greater knowledge and understanding
statue, a work of art, made in wood, stone, metal or other material, showing a person, an animal or some other form
impress, to affect deeply or strongly in mind or feelings
toy, a thing to play with especially for a child

After Kamante had become a Christian he was no longer afraid to touch a dead body.

Earlier in his life he had been afraid of it, and when a man, who had been carried up to the *terrace* by my house, died there, he would no more than the others ⁵ give a hand to carry him back. Why the Kikuyu, who personally have so little fear of death, should be so afraid to touch a dead body, while the white people, who are afraid to die, handle the dead easily, I do not know. Here once more you feel their reality to be dif- ¹⁰ ferent from ours.

Now the *terror* had disappeared from Kamante's heart. He did even show off a little here, as if to *boast* of the power of his God. It happened that I had opportunities to test his faith, and Kamante and I came to ¹⁵ carry three dead people between us, in the course of our life on the farm. One was an old white man who came to live on the farm, played a part in the life of it, and died there.

He was a countryman of mine, an old blind Dane by ²⁰ the name of Knudsen. One day when I was in Nairobi he came up to my car, introduced himself, and asked me to give him a house on my land, as he had no place in the world to live. I had at that time been reducing my staff of white people on the plantation, and had an ²⁵ empty house where he could stay, and he came out and lived on the farm for six months.

He was a strange figure to have on a highland farm:

terrace, an area beside a house, covered with flat stones, where one can sit
terror, extreme fear
boast, to talk about one's doings in a manner that shows too much self-importance

so much a creature of the sea that it was as if we had an old *albatros* with us. He was all broken by a hard life, and by disease and drink, with the unusual colouring of red-haired people gone white, as if he was marked by his own element and had been salted. He came of Danish fisherman stock and had been a *sailor*, and later one of the very early *pioneers* of Africa – whatever wind it was that blew him there.

Old Knudsen had tried a great many things in his life, preferably working with water or fish or birds, and had done well with none of them. At one time, he told me, he had owned a very fine fishing company on Lake Victoria, but during the war he had lost it all.

All this he told me on the occasions when he came up on a visit to my house, which he often did, for he was uncomfortable in his own house. The small native boys, whom I gave him as servants, ran away from him again and again, because he frightened them, running blindly towards them with his stick. But when he was in high spirits he would sit on my verandah over a cup of coffee and sing Danish songs to me with great energy. It was a pleasure for both him and me to speak Danish, so we exchanged remarks over unimportant happenings on the farm, just for the joy of talking.

Old Knudsen had in his broken body the simple wild heart of a small boy who burns with love of fighting. He was a good hater, always full of anger at nearly all the people and institutions with which he came in contact. It impressed me that Old Knudsen's soul should still –

albatros, a large sea-bird
sailor, one whose occupation is going to sea
pioneer, a person who is among the first to go into an area or a country to settle or work there

after a long hard life – cry out for opposition and trouble. It made me respect it.

A short time before he died he told me about a tremendous plan of his. It would make Old Knudsen a millionaire at last. He was going to lift, from the bottom of Lake Naivasha, the hundred tons of *guano* dropped there, from the time of the creation of the world, by the swimming-birds. In a last enormous effort he made a journey from the farm to Lake Naivasha, to study and work out the details of his plan which had all the elements dear to his heart: deep water, birds, hidden *treasure*.

From time to time he locked the door of his house, made off and disappeared for a while. It was most often, I think, when he had had news that an old friend, some other pioneer of the great past, had arrived in Nairobi. He always came back so terribly ill and worn out that he could hardly drag himself along or unlock his door. He then kept to himself for a couple of days.

On the day of his death he had been away for two weeks, and nobody on the farm was aware that he had come back. He had been on his way from his own house to mine, by a path which ran through the plantation, when he fell down and died. Kamante and I found him lying on the path late in the afternoon.

It was appropriate that it should be Kamante who found him, for, alone of all the Natives on the farm, he had taken an interest in Old Knudsen, as one person out of the ordinary in another. From time to time he

guano, bird droppings which can be used to make the soil richer for growing plants etc.
treasure, gold, silver or other valuable objects

had brought him eggs, and kept an eye on his totos, which had prevented them from running away altogether.

The old man lay on his back, his hat had rolled a little away when he fell, his eyes were not quite closed. In death he looked calm. There you are at last, Old Knudsen – I thought.

I wanted to carry him to his house, but I knew that it would be of no use to call in any of the Kikuyu who might be about or working in their own shambas close by, to help me; they would only run away immediately when they saw why I had called them. I ordered Kamante to run back to the house and fetch down Farah to help me.

"Why do you want me to run?"

"Well you see yourself," I said, "that I cannot carry the old Bwana alone, and you Kikuyu are fools, you are afraid of carrying a dead man."

Kamante let out a short silent laugh. "You again forget, Msabu," he said, "that I am a Christian."

He lifted the old man's feet while I held his head, and between us we carried him to his bungalow. From time to time we had to stop, lay him down, and rest; then Kamante stood up erect and looked straight down at Old Knudsen's feet, with what I think would have been the Scottish Mission manner in the presence of death.

As we had laid him on his bed, Kamante went about the room, and into the kitchen, in search of something to cover his face – he only found an old newspaper. "The Christians did that at the hospital," he explained to me.

A long time afterwards Kamante had great satisfaction out of the thought of this event. He would work with me in the kitchen, filled with secret pleasure, and suddenly break out laughing. "Do you remember, Msabu," he said, "the time when you had forgotten that I was a Christian, and thought that I would be 5 afraid to help you carry the **Msungu Mse**?" – the old white man.

Ater I went away I have heard from Kamante, and from my other houseboys in Africa. It is not more than a month since I had the last letter from him. But these 10 communications from Africa come to me in a strange unreal way, and are more like shadows than like news of a reality.

For Kamante cannot write, and he does not know English. When he, or my other people, take it into 15 their heads to send me their news, they go to one of the professional Indian or Native letter-writers who are sitting outside the post offices at their writing desk, and explain to them what shall be in the letter. The professional writers do not know much English either, and 20 can hardly be said to know how to write, but they themselves believe that they can. To show off their skill they make the letters more beautiful by adding a number of lines and drawings which make them difficult to read. From all these efforts come the sort of messages 25 that people got from the Oracle of Delphi*. There is a depth in the letters that touches you; you feel that there is some vital communication which has been heavy on the heart of the sender, which has made him walk a long way from the Kikuyu Reserve to the post 30

*in ancient Greece a place where one could ask the gods for advice

41

office. But it was covered in darkness. The cheap and dirty little sheet of paper that, when it comes to you, has travelled many thousand miles, seems to speak and speak, even to scream to you, but it tells you absolute-
5 ly nothing at all.

Kamante, however, in this as in most other ways, is different from other people. He puts three or four let-ters into the same *envelope*, and has them marked: 1st letter, 2nd letter, and so on. They all contain the same
10 things, repeated over and over.

Perhaps, in doing so, he wants to make a deeper impression on me. He had that way when talking when there was something that he particularly wanted me to understand or remember.

15 Kamante writes that he has been out of work for a long time. I was not surprised to hear that. I had edu-cated a royal cook and left him in a new colony. Where the great chef walked in deep thought, full of know-ledge, nobody sees anything but a little Kikuyu with
20 thin legs and a flat, *still* face.

What has Kamante got to say when he walks into Nairobi, takes up his stand before the Indian letter-writer, and explains a message to him that is to go round half the world? There is no order in the phrases
25 of the letter, but Kamante has in him a greatness of soul of which the people who knew him will still hear the note in the broken, disordered music.

This is a '2nd letter':

"I was not forget you Memsahib. Now all your ser-
30 vant they never glad because you was from the country.

envelope, letters are put into envelopes when they are sent
still, with little or no movement or sound; quiet and calm

42

If we was bird we fly and see you. Then we turn. Then your old farm it was good place for cow small *calf* black people. Now they had no anything cows goat sheep they has no anything. Now all bad people they enjoy in their heart because your old servant they come poor people now. Now God know in his heart all this to help sometime your servant." 5

And in '3rd letter' Kamante gives an example of the way in which the Native can say a beautiful thing to you, he writes: 10

"Write and tell us if you turn. We think you turn. Because why? We think that you shall never can forget us. Because why? We think that you remembered still all our face and our mother name."

A white man who wanted to say a pretty thing to you would write: "I can never forget you." The African says: "We do not think of you, that you can ever forget us." 15

2. A SHOOTING ACCIDENT ON THE FARM

The Shooting Accident

On the evening of the nineteenth of December I walked out of my house before going to bed, to see if 20 there was any rain coming. Many farmers in the highlands were, I believe, doing the same thing at that hour. Sometimes, in a lucky year, we would get a few heavy showers just round Christmas, and it was a great thing

| *calf/calves*, a young cow

43

for the young coffee, which had formed on the trees after the flowering in the short rains of October.

As I was standing before my house, looking at the sky above me bright with stars, a shot was fired, not far off. One shot. Then again the stillness of the night closed on all sides. I waited for some time for the second shot; nothing came, and as I looked again at the sky there was no rain coming either. So I went to bed, taking a book with me, and leaving the lamp to burn.

Two minutes later a motor cycle rounded the drive at a great speed and stopped in front of the house. Then someone knocked hard upon the long window of my sitting-room. I put some clothes on, took the lamp and went out. Outside was one of my managers, an American called Belknap. By this time, Farah had come from his house, and together we listened to Belknap's story.

He told us how peacefully and pleasantly the *tragedy* had started. His cook had had a day off, and in his absence a party had been given in the kitchen by the seven-year-old kitchen-toto, Kabero, a son of my old squatter and nearest neighbour on the farm, the old Kaninu. As, late in the evening, the company became very gay, Kabero had brought in his master's gun and, to his wild friends of the plains and shambas, had acted the part of a white man.

Belknap was a chicken farmer and kept a *shotgun* on his verandah to frighten away the *Serval cats*. Kabero, in the greatness of youth, had aimed straight in among his guests and pulled the *trigger*. Three of the children

---

tragedy, a terrible event causing much sadness
Serval-cat, a large African cat

44

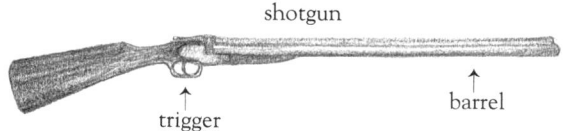

shotgun

trigger

barrel

had been slightly *wounded* and had run out of the kitchen in terror. Two were there now, badly hurt or dead.

While Belknap talked, my houseboys had come out, very silent; they went in again, and brought out a hur- 5 ricane lamp and the box with bandages and medicine. It would be a waste of time to try to start the car, so we ran as quickly as we could through the forest down to Belknap's house. As we ran, we could hear a number of short *shrieks* – death shrieks of a child. 10

The kitchen door was wide open. A gun was on the table beside a lamp and you could smell that it had been fired. There was blood all over the kitchen: I slipped in it on the floor.

I knew the children who had been shot, from the 15 plains of the farm, where they had herded their fathers' sheep. Wamai, Jogona's son, a lively little boy who had for some time been a pupil at the school, was lying on the floor between the door and the table. He was not dead, but not far from death. We lifted him aside, so 20 that we could move around. The child that shrieked was Wanyangerri, who had been the youngest of the party in the kitchen. He was sitting up, leaning for-

wound, an injury to part of the body, especially one caused by a weapon; to hurt, to injure
shriek, a loud sharp cry; to make such a sound

wards, towards the lamp; the blood *spouted* from his face – if one could still say face, for he must have stood straight in front of the *barrel* when it was fired and it had taken his lower *jaw* clean off. He held his arms out from his sides and moved them up and down, as the wings of a chicken go, after its head has been cut off.

When you are brought suddenly within the presence of such disaster – on the shooting-field or on the farm-yard – there seems to be but one piece of advice: that you should kill quickly and at any cost. And yet you know that you cannot kill, and your brain turns with fear. I put my hands to the child's head and pressed it in my *despair*, and, as if I had really killed him, he at the same moment stopped screaming, and sat erect with his arms hanging down, as if he was made of wood.

It is a difficult thing to bandage a patient whose face is half shot off. I had to lift the little boy onto Farah's knee, and make Farah hold his head in position for me, for if it fell forward I could not get the bandage placed, and if it fell back the blood ran down and filled his *throat*.

Then we lifted Wamai onto the table and held the lamp up to look at him. He had received the full charge of the gun in his throat. He did not *bleed* much, only a thin line of blood ran down from the corner of his mouth. It was surprising to see this Native child, who

spout, (of water and the like) to come out with great force from a narrow opening
barrel, see picture, page 45
despair, the state of having lost all hope
throat, the passage in the neck through which food and air are taken into the body
bleed, to lose blood

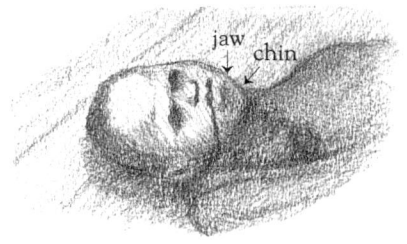

had been so full of life, so quiet now. I sent Farah to the house to get the car, for we had no time to waste in taking the children to hospital.

While we were waiting I asked about Kabero, the boy who had fired the shot. Belknap then told me a strange story about him. A couple of days earlier Kabero had bought an old pair of shorts from his master, and was to pay him a rupee from his wages. When the shot was fired, and Belknap ran out to the kitchen, Kabero was standing in the middle of the room with the smoking gun in his hand. He stared at Belknap for a second, and then he put his hand into the pocket of the very shorts that he had just bought and put on for the party, drew up a rupee and laid it on the table with his left hand, while with his right he threw the gun on the table. After having thus settled with the world, he was gone; he actually, although we did not know it at the moment, disappeared from the face of the earth. It was unusual behaviour for a Native, for they do not generally have debt on their mind, and in particular a debt to a white man. Perhaps to Kabero the moment had looked so much like the day of judgement that he felt he had got to play up to it; perhaps he was trying, in the hour of need, to make sure he had a friend.

47

At that time I had an old Overland car. I shall never write anything against her, for she served me well for many years. But she had to be pushed to start, and on this night it took a long time.

5   Visitors to my house had been telling me that the state of my road was very bad, and during the death-drive of that night I realized that they had been right. There were many deep holes. The distance to Nairobi seemed terribly long. I thought that I might have driven home to Denmark in the time that it took us.

10   The Native hospital of Nairobi lies on the hill just before you drive into the centre of the town. It was dark and we had much trouble to wake it up; in the end we got hold of an old doctor. As I helped to lift Wamai
15 out of the car I thought that he moved a little, but when we brought him into the brightly lit room in the hospital, he was dead. The old doctor kept waving his hand at him, saying: "He is dead." And then again at Wanyangerri, saying: "He is alive." At the time I did
20 not like his manner, but afterwards I felt as if fate itself in a number of big white coats, one after the other, had met us there at the entrance of the house, dealing out life and death *impartially*. I left the children there to their different fates.

25 Belknap, who had come with us on his motor bicycle, mostly to help us to push the car to start, should she stop on the road, now thought that we ought to report the accident to the police. So we drove into town to the River Road Police Station. There was no
30 white police officer present when we came, but in the end a young police officer arrived, straight from a party

---

   impartial, not favouring one person or thing more than another

48

and he took down the report. I felt cold in the night air. At last we could drive home.

While I was still in bed the next morning, I felt, by the deep silence outside the house, that there were many people around. I knew who they were: the old men of 5 the farm. I also knew what they wanted: they had come to inform me that they wished to set a **Kyama** on the death of the children.

A Kyama is an *assembly* of the *Elders* of the farm. It has been given authority by the Government to settle 10 the local differences among the squatters. The members of the Kyama gather round a crime, or an accident, and will sit over it for many weeks. I knew that now the old men would want to talk the whole matter over with me, and also that they would, if they could, in the end 15 make me come into their court to give the final judgement in the case. I did not want to take up an endless discussion of the tragedy of the night at this moment, and sent for my horse to get out and away from them.

Riding in the Reserve

I rode into the Masai Reserve. I had to cross the river 20 to get there; riding on, I got into the Game Reserve in a quarter of an hour. Here lay before me a hundred miles on horseback over grass in open land. There were no houses, only the Masai villages, but the Masai were

---

assembly, the meeting together of a group of people for a specific purpose
elders, people of greater age, experience and authority

away half the year with their herds. I turned to the animal world from the world of men; my heart was heavy with the tragedy of the night.

My relations with the Natives in the legal affairs of
5 the farm were of a strange nature. Since, before anything, I wanted peace on the land, I could not keep out of them. A *dispute* between squatters, which had not been properly settled, was like those sores that you get in Africa, and which they call veldt-sores: they heal on
10 the surface, but go on running underneath until you cut down to the bottom and clean them all through. The Natives themselves were aware of this, and if they really wanted a matter settled they would ask me to give judgement.

15 As I knew nothing of their laws, I needed their help to play the part given to me. This task my old men took upon themselves with *patience*. There would also be times when I refused to go along with it. When problems became difficult, I had to retire and take time to
20 think them over. This was always an effective move with the people of the farm, and I heard them, a long time afterwards, talk with respect of the case that had been so deep that no one could look through it in less than a week. One can always impress a Native by wast-
25 ing more time over a matter than he does himself.

The ideas of justice of Europe and Africa are not the same. To the African there is but one way of *counterbalancing* the disasters of existence, it shall be done by

dispute, lack of agreement
patience, the power to wait calmly, to bear trouble or suffering without getting angry
to counterbalance, to act as a counterbalance, that is a weight or force that balances another by having the opposite effect

50

replacement; he does not look for the *motive* of an action. Whether you lie in wait for your enemy and cut his throat in the dark; or you cut down a tree, and a thoughtless stranger passes by and is killed: to the Native mind it is the same thing. A loss has been 5 brought upon the community and must be made up for, somewhere, by somebody. He will think deeply and for a long time about the method by which crime or disaster must be made up in sheep and goats – time does not count to him. 10

As I was riding back to the farm, on crossing the river, I met a party of Kaninu's sons, three young men and a boy. When I stopped them and asked for news of their brother Kabero, they spoke slowly. Kabero, they said, had not come back, and nothing had been heard of him 15 since he had run away last night. They were now certain that he was dead. He would either have killed himself in his despair – since the idea of *suicide* comes very naturally to all Natives, and even to Native children – or he had been lost in the bush and the wild animals 20 had eaten him. His brothers had been out looking for him in all directions; they were now on their way into the Reserve to try to find him there.

When I came up the river-bank on my own land, I turned and looked out over the plain; my land was 25 higher up than the land of the Reserve. There was no sign of life anywhere on the plain, except for the zebras a long way off. As the young men came out of the bush

replacement, the act of letting someone or something take the place of another
motive, that which causes someone to act in a particular way; a reason (for committing a crime)
suicide, the act of killing oneself

on the other side of the river, they went on quickly. They seemed fairly confident about their direction, but what would it be? In their search for the lost child, their only guide would be the vultures that are always
5 hanging in the sky above a dead body on the plain. This would be only a very small body, not much for the vultures to eat. There would not be many of them to spot it, nor would they be out looking for a very long time.
10 All this was sad to think of. I rode home.

Wamai

I went to the Kyama with Farah. I always had Farah with me in my dealings with the Kikuyu, for while he showed *but* little sense where his own quarrels were concerned, and like all Somali would lose his head
15 when his tribal feelings came up, about other people's differences he showed good judgement. He was also my *interpreter*.

I knew before I arrived at the assembly that the chief object of the proceedings would be to make Kaninu pay
20 as much as possible. He would see his sheep driven away to all sides, some to *indemnify* the families of the dead and wounded children, some to maintain the

---

but, here, only
interpreter, a person who hears something in one language and immediately changes it into another language
indemnify, to pay somebody a sum of money (here a number of sheep) for damage suffered

Kyama. I was against this from the beginning. For Kaninu, I thought, had lost his son just as the other fathers, and the fate of his child seemed to me the most *tragic* of the lot. Wamai was dead and out of it, and Wanyangerri was in hospital, where people were looking after him, but Kabero had been abandoned by all, and nobody knew where his bones lay.

Kaninu was ideal for the part of the ox *fattened* for the feast. He was one of my biggest squatters; on my squatter-list he is down for thirty-five head of cattle, five wives, and sixty goats. I and Kaninu had had many angry arguments. I had indeed been threatening to turn him off the farm because of his dealings with the Masai. Kaninu was on good terms with the neighbouring Masai tribe, and had married four or five of his daughters off to them. The Kikuyu themselves told me how in the old times the Masai had thought it beneath them to marry a Kikuyu. But in our days the strange dying nation, to delay its final disappearance, has had to come down in its *pride*. The Masai women have no children, but the Kikuyu have, so their women are in demand with the tribe. All Kaninu's children were good-looking people, and he had brought back a number of young cows across the border of the Reserve in exchange for his young daughters. More than one old Kikuyu in this period became rich in the same way. The big Chief of the Kikuyu, Kinanjui, had sent, I was told, more than twenty of his daughters to the Masai, and had got over a hundred head of cattle in return for them.

tragic, marked by a sense of tragedy
fatten, to become or make something or somebody fat
pride, a (too) high opinion of oneself or respect for oneself

But a year ago the Masai Reserve had been put under *quarantine* for foot-and-mouth disease, and no stock could be taken out of it. This was a serious problem for Kaninu. For the Masai are nomads, and those cows in
5 their herds which lawfully belonged to Kaninu were dragged all over the land and would at times be a hundred miles away, where nobody knew what was happening to them. The Masai are *unscrupulous* cattle-dealers with anyone, and more so with the Kikuyu for
10 whom they have no respect. So the old Kikuyu had his cattle moved at night across the water to my farm. This was very bad behaviour on his part, for the quarantine regulations are among those which the Natives understand; they think highly of them. Had these cows been
15 found on my land, the farm itself would have been put under quarantine. I therefore set out watchmen down by the river to catch Kaninu's men, and on moonlit nights there had been many great dramatic *ambushes*.

Jogona, the father of the child Wamai who had been
20 killed, was, on the other hand, a poor man. He had but one old wife, and all he owned in the world were three goats. I knew him well. He was a friendly, old man and pleasant to talk to, and whenever he looked at me he laughed. He now seemed very pleased to see me at the
25 Kyama.

Besides myself, at least one other member of the assembly knew that its purpose was to rob Kaninu of his

quarantine, a period of time when an animal or a person that has or may have a disease is kept away from others in order to prevent the disease from spreading
unscrupulous, without moral principles
ambush, the act of waiting in a hidden position for somebody in order to catch them

54

wealth: this was Kaninu himself. The other old men sat around, paying close attention to the proceedings. Kaninu, on the ground, had drawn his big *cloak* of goatskin over his head; from time to time he gave out under it a *whine* or *whimper*, like that of a dog which is exhausted by howling and is just keeping its *misery* alive.

The old men wanted to begin with the case of the wounded child Wanyangerri, because it gave them endless opportunity for arguing. How would his family be indemnified if he died? If he would not be able to talk again? I asked Farah to tell them that I would not discuss this matter until I had been in Nairobi and had seen the doctor at the hospital. They hid their disappointment and got their arguments on the next point ready.

It was up to the Kyama, I told them through Farah, to get this case settled quickly, and they should not sit over it for the rest of their lives. It was clear that it was not a murder case, but a bad accident.

The Kyama listened to my speech with attention, but as soon as it was finished they told me that they did not agree.

"Msabu, we know nothing," they said. "But here we see that you do not know enough either, and we understand only a little of what you say to us. It was Kaninu's son who fired the shot. Otherwise how would he be

---

cloak, a type of coat that closes at the neck and hangs loosely from the shoulders
whine, a long sharp cry, especially one made by a dog or a child
whimper, (of a person or an animal) to make a series of low weak sad cries, with fear or pain
exhausted, very tired
misery, great suffering

the only one not hurt by it? If you want to hear more about it Mauge here will tell you. His son was there and had one of his ears shot off."

Mauge was one of the wealthiest squatters and his word had weight, although he spoke very slowly and from time to time had to stop and think. "Msabu," he said. "My son told me: the boys all held the gun the one after the other and pointed it at Kabero. But he would not explain to them how to shoot with it, no, he would not explain it at all. In the end he took the gun back, and at the same moment it shot, it wounded all the children and killed Wamai, Jogona's son. This is exactly how it happened."

"I knew that already," I said, "and it is what is called bad luck, and an accident. Kaninu will pay Jogona a number of sheep to make up for the loss. But everybody also knows that Kaninu's son was not a bad child and did not mean to kill Wamai. Kaninu will not pay as many sheep as if that had been the case. The boy was clever in school and good in all other ways, it is a very bad thing for Kaninu to lose him."

There was a long pause, not a sound in the ring. At the end of it Kaninu, as if he suddenly remembered a forgotten pain or duty, gave out a long howl.

"Memsahib," said Farah, "let these Kikuyu now name the figure that they have in their hearts." He spoke in Swahili to me, so that the assembly should understand him, and succeeded in making them feel uncomfortable, for a precise figure is something no Native likes to give. Farah let his eyes run all round the circle and suggested: "One hundred." A hundred sheep was an enormous number, which nobody would seriously have thought of. A silence fell upon the Kyama.

56

The old men did not like the Somali's joke. A very old man whispered "Fifty" but the figure seemed to carry no weight.

After a moment Farah himself quickly said "Forty" in the manner of the experienced cattle-trader, at home with figures and stock. They began to talk in a lively manner among themselves. They would now need time to think it over and talk about it, but all the same a basis for negotiations had been laid. When we were at home again Farah said to me with confidence: "I think that these old men will take forty sheep from Kaninu."

After about a week of sittings of the Kyama, it was finally decided that forty sheep should be paid by Kaninu to Jogona.

Two weeks later Farah gave me fresh news of the case.

Three old Kikuyu from Nyeri, he told me, had arrived at the farm the day before. They had heard of the case in their huts up at Nyeri and had walked from there to appear on the scene. They claimed that Wamai was not the son of Jogona but was their late brother's son, and that they should have the sheep.

I smiled and remarked to Farah that this was just like the Kikuyu of Nyeri. No, said Farah thoughtfully, he believed that they were right. Jogona had indeed come from Nyeri to the farm six years ago, and from what Farah had gathered, Wamai was not Jogona's son, "and never had been," Farah said. It was, he went on, a great stroke of luck to Jogona that he had, two days before, been handed over twenty-five of his forty sheep. Otherwise Kaninu would have let them go off to Nyeri so as to save himself the pain. But Jogona would have to

57

look out still, for the Nyeri Kikuyu were not easy to shake off. They were now staying on the farm and threatened to bring the case before the *D.C.*

In this way I was prepared for the appearance, a few days later, before my house, of the Nyeri people who belonged to a low class of Kikuyu, and had all the look of three dirty *hyenas* that had *slunk* one hundred and fifty miles on Wamai's blood-track. With them came Jogona who looked very unhappy. The difference in the attitude of the parties probably came from the fact that the Nyeri Kikuyu had nothing to lose, while Jogona had twenty-five sheep. The three men sat immovable on the stones. I had no sympathy with their cause, for, whatever the circumstances were, they had taken no interest in the dead child while he had lived, and I was sorry for Jogona who had behaved well at the Kyama, and had, I believed, been very sad over Wamai's death. Jogona, when I questioned him, was so worried that it was impossible to understand what he was saying, and we got no further on this occasion.

But two days later Jogona came back early in the morning, when I was at my typewriter, and asked me to write down for him the account of his relations to the dead child and its family. He wanted to take the report before the D.C. at Dagoretti. Jogona's very simple and serious manner impressed me. It was obvious that he was looking upon his decision as upon a great and difficult project which was not without danger.

D.C., the District Commissioner, that is the government's representative in a district
hyena, an animal found in Africa and Asia that eats the flesh of dead animals
slink, to move as if one feels guilty, or does not want to be seen

I wrote his statement down for him. It took a long time, for it was a long report of events more than six years ago, and in themselves extremely complicated. Jogona, as he was going through it, continually had to break off his story to think things over. He was, most 5 of the time, holding his head with both hands, at moments hitting the top of it as if to shake out the facts. Once he went and leaned his face against the wall, as the Kikuyu women do when they are giving birth to their children. 10

I took a copy of the report; I still have it. It began:

"At the time when Waweru Wamai, of Nyeri, was about to die he had two wives. The one wife had three daughters; after Waweru's death she married another man. The other wife, Waweru had not yet paid for alto- 15 gether: he still owed her father two goats for her..." It went on in this way, and dragged the reader through a long story of Kikuyu conditions and relations:

"This wife had one small child by the name of Wamai. At that time he was very sick. Waweru was 20 very fond of his wife and of her child, and when he was dying he was very worried because he did not know what would become of her when he was dead. He therefore sent for his friend Jogona Kanyagga, who lived not far away. Jogona Kanyagga owed Waweru, at 25 this time, three shillings for a pair of shoes. Waweru now suggested to him that they should make an agreement. Jogona should take over the dying friend's wife and child, and pay to her father the two goats that were still due to him from the sum of her purchase price. 30

From this point the report became a list of *expenses*,

expense, the cost of something; the spending of money

59

which Jogona had brought upon himself through the adoption of the child Wamai. He had, he stated, purchased an extraordinarily good medicine for Wamai just after he had taken him over. The list named sever-
5 al other occasions upon which Jogona had paid for Wamai. At the end of it, it appeared that he had forgotten that the child whom he had now lost had not been his own. He was shaken by the arrival and the claim of the three Nyeri people.
10   When Jogona had at last come to the end of his story, and I had got it all down, I told him that I was now going to read it to him. As I read out his own name, "And he sent for Jogona Kanyagga, who was his friend and who lived not far away," he gave me a *flaming*
15 glance, so filled with laughter that it changed the old man into a boy, into the very image of youth. Again, as I had finished the document and was reading out his name that I had typed below his *thumbmark*, the vital direct glance was repeated, this time deeper and
20 calmer, with a new dignity.

thumbmark

Such a glance did Adam give the Lord when he formed him out of the dust and breathed life into him, and man became a living soul. I had created him and shown him himself: Jogona Kanyagga of life everlast-

---

| *flaming*, here, showing strong feelings

ing. When I handed him the paper, he took it with very great respect, folded it up, put it in a corner of his cloak and kept his hand over it. He could not afford to lose it, for his soul was in it, and it was the proof of his existence.

The statement proved very useful to him, for when the D.C. had read it, he refused to consider the case of the Nyeri people, who walked back to their own village with empty hands and very angry.

The document now became Jogona's great treasure. Jogona made a little leather bag for it and hung it round his neck. From time to time, mostly on Sunday mornings he would suddenly appear at my door, lift the bag off and take out the paper to have it read to him. At each reading his face took on the same expression of deep religious triumph, and afterwards he carefully folded it up and put it back in the bag. The importance of the account did not become less but grew with time, as if to Jogona the greatest wonder about it was that it did not change. The past, that had been so difficult to bring to memory, and that had probably seemed to be changing every time it was thought of, had here been caught and defined exactly. It had become history.

Wanyangerri

When I was next in Nairobi, I went to see Wanyangerri in the Native Hospital. As I had so many squatter families on my land, I was hardly ever without a patient in there.

Wanyangerri was in such a bad state that I thought the best thing for him would be to die. He was frightened of everything, *weeping* all the time I was with him, and *begging* to be taken back to the farm.

It was a week before I came again. He was then calm and received me with dignity. He was, however, very
5 pleased to see me, for he could today tell me, with confidence, though the words came out with great difficulty, that he had been killed the day before, and was going to be killed again in a few days' time.

The doctor who treated Wanyangerri had been to
10 the war in France*, and had *patched up* many people's faces; he took trouble with him and made a success of the job. He put in a metal band for a jawbone and joined it onto the bones left in the face, and he had picked up bits of torn flesh and *stitched* them together
15 to make a sort of *chin* for him. When at the end of the treatment the bandages came off, the face of the child was much changed, and looked strange, like the head of a *lizard*, because it had got no chin. But he was able to eat in a normal way. All this took many months.

lizard

20 During all this time Wanyangerri's case was waiting. His people sometimes came and asked me how he was

weep, to cry
beg, to ask in a very serious way
*World War I (1914-1918)
patch up, to place a piece of material over a hole or a damaged or worn place to cover it
stitch, see picture, page 83
chin, see picture, page 47

getting on, but they had all, except his little brother, been too afraid to go in to see him. Kaninu also came round to my house to ask for news of the child. A couple of months after the accident, Farah informed me of a new development in the case. 5

"Memsahib," he said, "the Kabero." This was the programme then. I waited for what was to follow.

After a pause Farah took up the subject again. "You think, Memsahib," he said, "that Kabero is dead and has been eaten by the hyenas. He is not dead. He is 10 with the Masai."

In two minds I asked him how he knew of this. "Oh, I know," he said, "Kaninu has got too many girls married to Masai. When Kabero could not think of anybody who would help him except the Masai, he ran out 15 to his sister's husband. It is true that he had a bad time, he sat all night in a tree with hyenas waiting around it. Now he is living with the Masai. There is a rich old Masai, who has got many hundred cows, who has no children himself and wants to have Kabero. Kaninu 20 knows of all this very well, and has been out to talk it over with the Masai many times. But he is afraid to tell you, he believes that if the white people know of it, Kabero will be hanged in Nairobi. Still, this Kabero, he will come back to the farm when he grows up, for he 25 will not want to live like the Masai, always going from one place to the other. The Kikuyu are too *lazy* for that. But Kaninu's wife is sorry to lose her son for so many years."

I did not send for Kaninu, for I did not know 30 whether to believe what Farah had told me or not, but

---

lazy, unwilling to work; doing as little work as possible

when he next came to my house I went out to talk to him. "Kaninu," I asked him, "is Kabero alive? Is he with the Masai?" You will never find a Native unprepared for any action of yours, and Kaninu immediately
5 burst out weeping over his lost child. I listened to him and looked at him for a little while. "Kaninu," I said again, "bring Kabero here. He will not be hanged. His mother shall keep him with her on the farm." Kaninu had stopped his weeping to listen. "Kaninu," I said,
10 "when Kabero wants to return to the farm he can do so and no harm shall come to him. But you must bring him up here to me yourself at that time." Kaninu fell dead silent, turned and walked away sadly as if he had now lost his last friend in the world.

15 I may as well tell you here that Kaninu remembered, and did as he had been told. Five years later, when I had almost forgotten the whole affair, I found him standing outside my house one day. "Kabero is back," he said. By that time I had learned the art of the pause,
20 I did not say a word. "My son Kabero has come back to the farm," he repeated. I asked: "He is back from the Masai?" Immediately, because he had made me speak, Kaninu took it that I had accepted Kabero back on the farm. "Yes, Msabu, yes, he is back from the Masai," he
25 said, "he has come back to work for you."
   By that time the government had introduced the **Kipanda**, and each individual Native in the country had to register with the police. So we would now have to call a police officer out from Nairobi to make a law-
30 ful *inhabitant* of the farm out of Kabero. Kaninu and I

| *inhabitant*, a person living in a place

appointed the day.

On that day, Kaninu and his son arrived a long time before the police officer. Kaninu presented Kabero to me in a friendly manner, but at heart he was a little frightened of his newly found son. He had reason to be so, for the Masai Reserve had had from the farm a small lamb, and now gave us back a young lion. Kabero must have had Masai blood in him, the habits and the hard life of the Masai could not in themselves have caused the change. Here he stood, a Masai from head to foot.

A Masai *warrior* is a fine sight. Those young men have the intelligence of being true to their own nature. Their style is not an assumed manner, it has grown from the inside, and is an expression of the race and its history, and their weapons and colourful clothes are part of their being. Kabero stood in front of us, holding his head like a Masai, with his chin stretched forward, an object to be studied, such as a statue is, a figure which is to be seen, but which itself does not see.

The police officer from Nairobi was a young man just arrived from England. He told me that he thought the old case of the shooting accident ought to be taken up in Nairobi. Kaninu turned to wood. He looked at me. "That will mean years of your life and mine," I said. In the end it was found that the case was too old to be taken up, and nothing more was done about it, except that Kabero was now registered on the farm.

But all these things were to happen only a long time later. For five years Kabero was dead to the farm, *wan-*

---

warrior, a person who fights in a battle

65

dering with the Masai.

At that time things were happening in my life, that took my thoughts off Kaninu and his fate, and left, in my mind, the general affairs of the farm in the back-
5 ground like that distant mountain of Kilimanjaro. The Natives would afterwards refer to those periods as to times when I had been away. "That big tree fell down," they said. "My child died, while you were with the white people."

10 When Wanyangerri was well enough to leave hospital, I brought him back to the farm, and from then only saw him from time to time, at a **Ngoma*** or on the plains.

A few days after his return his father, Wainaina, and
15 his grandmother presented themselves at my house. Wanyangerri, his father told me, could not eat maize because of his jaw, they were poor people and they had got no milking cow. Would I not, till Wanyangerri's case was settled, allow him a little milk from my cows?
20 Otherwise they did not see how they were to keep the child alive until the time when his *indemnification* should come through. Farah was away and in his absence I agreed to let Wanyangerri have a bottle of milk a day. I told my houseboys that they should let
25 him have it every morning, but they did not seem to like the arrangement.

Two or three weeks passed; then one evening Kaninu came to the house. He suddenly stood in the room where I was reading by the fire after dinner. As the

---

wander, to walk around in an area or go from place to place
*a big native dance
indemnification, payment for damage suffered

66

Natives generally prefer a discussion to take place out-side the house, the manner in which he shut the door behind him prepared me for surprising communica-tions. But the first surprise was that Kaninu said noth-ing, and the room, with Kaninu in it, remained silent. 5 The big old Kikuyu was looking very ill, he hung upon his stick, there seemed to be no body inside his cloak.

When at last he began to speak it was only to state, slowly and sadly, that he thought things were bad. A little later he added that he had now paid over ten 10 sheep to Wainaina. And now Wainaina, he went on, wanted a cow and and calf from him as well, and he was going to give them to him. Why had he done that, I asked him, when no judgement had yet been given? Kaninu did not answer, he did not even look at me. 15 There were tears in his eyes. That was a strange thing and I wondered what had been happening on the farm while my thoughts had been elsewhere. When Kaninu had gone I sent for Farah and asked him.

Farah did not like to speak about Native affairs, as if 20 they were beneath him. In the end he told me, all the time looking out of the window at the stars, that at the bottom of Kaninu's loss of heart was Wainaina's moth-er, who was a *witch* and had put a *spell* on him.

"But, Farah, " I said, "Kaninu, surely, is much too old 25 and *wise* to believe in a spell."

"No," said Farah slowly. "No, Memsahib. For this old Kikuyu woman can really do these things, I think."

---

witch, woman believed to have evil magic powers over others
spell, words which when spoken are thought to have power that cannot be explained
wise, having or showing good judgement based on knowledge and experience

The old woman had told Kaninu that it would have
been better for his cows if Kaninu had given them to
Wainaina at the beginning. Now Kaninu's cows were
going blind, one after another, and Kaninu's heart was
5 breaking.

Farah spoke of Kikuyu *witchcraft* in a dry, concerned
manner, as of foot-and-mouth disease on the farm,
which we ourselves would not catch, but by which we
might lose our cattle.

10 "This old woman is mean," I thought in Swahili,
"she uses her arts to make Kaninu's cows blind, and she
leaves it to me to keep her grandchild alive, on a bottle of milk a day, from my own cows." I had by now
become used to the idea of witchcraft, it seemed a rea-
15 sonable thing in Africa.

I thought: "This accident and the things which have
come from it, are getting into the blood of the farm,
and it is my fault. I must call in fresh forces. I know
what I will do, I will send for Kinanjui."

A Kikuyu Chief

The big Chief Kinanjui lived about nine miles north-
east of the farm, in the Kikuyu Reserve near the
French Mission, and ruled over more than a hundred
thousand Kikuyu. He was a clever old man, with much
real greatness.

20 Kinanjui was a friend of mine, and had been helpful
to me on many occasions. His village was much bigger

witchcraft, the use of magic powers, especially evil ones

than any other I had seen, for in his position of chief, Kinanjui had given himself fully to the joys of marriage. The village was alive with wives of his of all ages and their children. Kinanjui had told me once that he had at that moment fifty-five sons. 5

Sometimes the old chief would come walking over to my farm in a *gorgeous* cloak, accompanied by two or three white-haired old men from his council and a few of his warrior-sons, on a friendly visit, or to take a rest from governmental affairs. He would then pass the 10 afternoon in one of the verandah chairs that had been carried out on the lawn for him, smoking the cigars that I sent out to him. My houseboys and the squatters, when they had news of his arrival, came and grouped themselves there, and told him about the happenings 15 on the farm, the whole company forming a sort of political club under the tall trees. I sometimes had a chair moved out for a talk with him, and on these occasions Kinanjui sent everybody else away.

I now sent a runner to Kinanjui's village and 20 explained to him the whole affair of the shooting. I asked him to come over to the farm to put an end to it. I suggested that we should give Wainaina the cow and the calf of which Kaninu had talked, and then let the whole matter end at that. I was looking forward to 25 Kinanjui's arrival, for he had the quality, which everyone values in a friend, of being effective.

One afternoon, as I was riding back to my house, I just caught sight of a car that came along at a terrible speed, rounding the drive on two wheels. It was a shin- 30 ing, red car. I knew it, it belonged to the American

gorgeous, very beautiful; wonderful

Consul of Nairobi, and I wondered what business it was which brought the consul to my house at such speed. But as I was getting off my horse at the back of the house, Farah came out to tell me that Chief Kinanjui
5 had arrived. He had come in his own car, which he had bought from the American Consul the day before. He did not want to get out till I had seen him in it.

I found Kinanjui sitting in the car, erect and immovable as a statue, staring straight in front of him while I
10 *paid* him my *compliments* on the car. He then collected his big cloak around him and stepped out of the car which one of his sons had been driving. We sat down outside the house. Farah took up his stand on my right hand, and from there kept an eye on the Kikuyu, who
15 had been gathering around the house, and who kept coming in as the news of Kinanjui's arrival spread on the farm.

Farah's attitude to the Natives of the country was interesting. Like the figures of the Masai warriors, it
20 had not been made yesterday, or the day before; it was the product of many centuries. The forces that had built it up had constructed great buildings in stone as well, but they had turned to dust a long time ago.

When you first come to the country, landing at
25 Mombasa, you will see grey stone *ruins* of houses and

---

consul, an official appointed by a state to live in a foreign country. A consul's job is to help people from his own country who are travelling or living abroad
to pay somebody a compliment, to express the feeling or opinion that something is good
ruin, the parts of a building or town that remain after it has fallen down or been destroyed

minaret

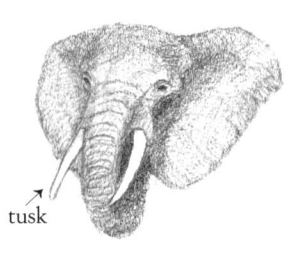

tusk

minarets. The same sort of ruins can be found all the way up the coast, at Takaunga, Kalifi, and Lamu. They are what remains of the towns of the ancient Arab traders in *ivory* and *slaves*.

As these great *merchants* grew rich, they brought 5 their *harems* with them to Mombasa and Kalifi and ramained in their villas by the ocean, while they sent their *expeditions* up into the highlands.

Their wealth came from the wild hard country, the burnt dry plains, and unknown waterless stretches, 10 from the land of the small, strong-smelling wild flowers of the black soil. Here, upon the roof of Africa, wan-

---

ivory, a bone-like material of which the elephant's *tusks* are made
slave, a person who is legally owned by somebody and is forced to work for them
merchant, a person involved in a trade or commercial activity
harem, the part of a Muslim house reserved for the women; the women living there
expedition, an organized journey with a particular aim

dered the heavy, *majestic* bearer of the ivory. He was followed and shot with *poisoned arrows* by the small dark Wanderobos, and with guns by the Arabs, all for his long tusks, that the merchants were waiting for at Zanzibar.

Here, also, little bits of forest soil were cleared, burned, and planted with sweet potatoes and maize, by a peace-loving nation which wished to be left to itself, and which, with the ivory, was in great demand on the market.

The Arabs came, with no respect for death, with their minds, on astronomy, *algebra*, and their harems. With them came their half-brothers the Somali, *greedy* and *quarrelsome*, and the Swahili went along with them.

Up country they were met by the Natives of the highlands. The Masai came, silent, like tall narrow black shadows, with *spears* and heavy *shields*, to sell their brothers.

The different brothers must have sat together up here and talked. Farah told me that in the old times, before the Somali brought their own women down from Somaliland, their young men were only allowed to marry the daughters of the Masai, out of all the tribes of the country. The Masai, Farah told me, had never

majestic, grand; royal; showing great dignity
poison, to harm or kill a living thing with poison, a stuff causing death if taken into the body
algebra, a branch of mathematics in which letters are used to represent quantities
greedy, full of desire for wealth, power, etc for oneself
quarrelsome, who likes starting quarrels

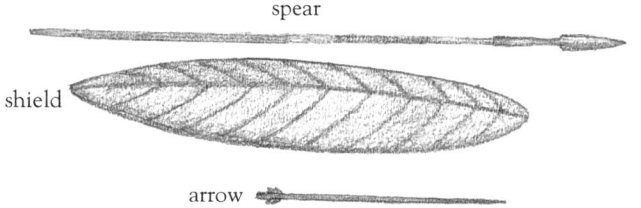

spear

shield

arrow

been slaves. They cannot be made slaves, they cannot
even be put in prison. They die in prison within three
months if they are put there, so according to the
English law of the country they are not put in prison
but have to pay a *fine* if they break the law.   5

The Somali had their own position. They are not
good at being on their own, if they are left to themselves they will waste much time and blood over their
tribal moral system. But they are fine seconds-in-com-
mand, and perhaps the Arab capitalists often put them   10
in charge of the the difficult transports while they
remained behind in Mombasa. Therefore their relation
to the Natives was nearly exactly that of the sheepdog
to the sheep. They watched them without ever getting
tired. Would they die before the coast was reached?   15
Would they escape? The Somali have a good sense of
money and values, they would have given up food and
sleep for their charges. This habit is still in their blood.

The sheep themselves, the *patient* nations, with no
power and no one on earth to protect them, survived   20
their fate with their enormous sense of *resignation.* They

fine, a sum of money that must be paid by someone who breaks the
law; here a number of cattle to be paid
patient, having the ability to accept delay or suffering
resignation, the ability to suffer patiently that which cannot be changed

73

were friends with God in foreign countries, and in chains. They also kept up a certain self-respect: they knew that they were the central figures in the affair, they were valuable goods. They did not think highly of
5 the sheepdogs. The Kikuyu on the farm at times had a *flippant* manner towards Farah, as a lamb may jump up in the face of the sheepdog just to make him get up and run.

Farah and Kinanjui met here, the sheepdog and the
10 old ram. Farah stood up erect in his red and blue *turban*, his Arab *waistcoat* and Arab silk *robe*. Kinanjui was spreading himself on the stone seat, *naked* but for the cloak on his shoulders, an old Native, a bit of the soil of the African highlands.

15 The big meeting which was to settle the case of the shooting accident began in a peaceful spirit. The people of the farm were all pleased to see Kinanjui. The oldest squatters got up and came to exchange a few remarks with him, then walked back and took their
20 seats on the grass. Kaninu was present, in the middle of his large family. Wainaina and his mother came along and sat a little apart from the others.

I told the people that the matter between Kaninu and Wainaina had been settled and put down on paper.
25 Kinanjui had come over to *certify* it. Kaninu was to give Wainaina a cow with a calf, and with that the affair should be ended.

Kaninu and Wainaina had been informed of the decision beforehand, and Kaninu was told to have the

flippant, not showing a serious attitude or sufficient respect
naked, not wearing any clothes
certify, to declare something to be true or legally binding

turban

waistcoast

robe

cow and calf ready. When I had read out the agreement I told Kaninu to bring the cow. Kaninu got up
and waved to two of his sons, who were holding the
cow behind the boys' huts. The ring opened while the
cow and calf were slowly led into the middle of it. ⁵

At the same moment the atmosphere of the meeting
changed in a dramatic way.

There is nothing in the world which is more interesting and important to a Kikuyu than a cow with a
baby calf. Wainaina's mother broke into a long whine ¹⁰
and shook a dry arm and finger at the cow. Wainaina
joined her. He raised his voice to heaven, and breaking
in his speech, as if someone else were speaking through

him. He could not accept the cow; she was the oldest in Kaninu's herd, and the calf that she had now got with her, that surely was the last which she would ever bear.

5 The *clan* of Kaninu cried out and cut him short, naming all the good qualities of the cow. The people of the farm did not have it in them to remain silent where a cow and calf were being discussed. Everyone present gave his opinion. The high voices of the old women 10 joined in and the young men shouted short deadly remarks at one another in deep voices.

I looked towards Farah and he looked back at me, but like a man in a dream. I saw that he was about to enter the battle. For the Somali are themselves stock-
15 owners and cattle traders. Kaninu threw me a glance like a *drowning* man who is finally carried away by the *current*. I took a look at the cow that was standing patiently in the middle of the excitement that she had created. I thought that she did have, somehow, the 20 look of an old cow.

At last I turned my eyes to Kinanjui. I do not know whether he had been looking at the cow at all. He sat immovable, having turned his side to the screaming crowd, with the true face of a king. I do not think that 25 Kinanjui could have spoken or moved without making things worse; as it was he kept sitting down to calm them. Not everybody could have done it.

Little by little the excitement died down, people stopped screaming and began to talk in an everyday

clan, a group of families, coming from the same father originally
drown, to die in water because one is unable to breathe
current, a movement of water going in a certain direction in a larger body of water

manner; in the end they fell silent one by one. Wainaina's mother, when she thought that nobody was watching her, came forward a few steps on her stick to have a closer look at the cow. Farah turned and came back to civilization, with a little mocking smile. *5*

When everything was quiet we made the parties in the case come to the table and press their thumbmarks down on the document of agreement. Wainaina whimpered a little when he set his thumb to the paper, as if it was burning him. *10*

3. VISITORS TO THE FARM

Big Dances

We had many visitors to the farm. In pioneer countries *hospitality* is a *necessity* of life not for the travellers alone but also for the settlers. A visitor is a friend, he brings news which is bread to the hungry minds in lonely places. *15*

When Denys Finch-Hatton came back after one of his long expeditions, he felt a great need to talk, and found me on the farm feeling the same way. So we sat at the dinner-table into the small hours of the morning, talking of all the things we could think of. White peo- *20*

---

hospitality, friendly treatment of guests or strangers in one's own home
necessity, the state of being necessary; circumstances that force one to do something

ple, who for a long time live alone with Natives, get into the habit of saying what they mean, and when they meet again their conversation keeps the same tone.

The greatest social functions on the farm were the **Ngomas** – the big Native dances. On these occasions we *entertained* up to fifteen hundred or two thousand guests. We did not offer them much, but I sometimes asked the D.C.'s permission for my squatters to make **tembu**, a deadly drink, made from sugar. It was the young dancers that made it such a splendid event. They were untouched by foreign influence, and concentrated upon the fire within themselves. Only one thing did they demand from the outside world: a space of level ground to dance on. This was to be found near my house: the big lawn was flat under the trees, and the square in the forest between my boys' huts had been laid out level. For this reason the farm was highly thought of by the young people of the country, and the invitation to my dances much valued.

When the news of the Ngoma had spread widely enough we would even see here the young ladies of Nairobi – the **Malaya**, a pretty word in Swahili – arriving in style, in Ali Khan's mule-carts, and looking, when seated, like large flowers on the grass. The respectable young girls on the farm in their traditional dress, took up their position close to them, and openly discussed their clothes and manners, but the beauties of the town, cross-legged, remained as quiet as glass-eyed dolls of dark wood, and smoked their small cigars. A great number of children ran from one ring to another,

entertain, to receive somebody as a guest

78

trying to learn, or were carried away to form little danc-
ing-rings of their own further away on the lawn.

The Kikuyu, when going to a Ngoma, *rub* themselves all over with a particular kind of pale red *chalk*.
It gives them a strange *blond* look. In it the young peo- 5
ple look like statues cut in rock. The young men are
naked for a Ngoma, but make much of their hairstyles,
putting chalk on their head. During my last years in
Africa, the Government *forbade* people to put chalk on
their head. 10

The daytime Ngomas were very noisy affairs. The
dancing music from *flutes* and *drums* often drowned in
the shouts from the audience. The dancing girls them-

flute

← drum

rub (something on), to put on a soft material by moving the hand for-
wards and backwards on a surface
chalk, a type of soft white rock used to write on a blackboard, for
example
blond, (of a person) having pale golden hair
forbid, to order somebody not to do something

79

selves gave out a strange, long cry when, in one of the figures performed by male dancers, a **Moran** made a jump, or swung his spear over his head in an exceptionally fine manner. Sitting on the grass, the old peo-
5 ple continued to keep up a conversation. The sun sank lower, and the supply of tembu as well.

But the Ngomas at night were set about in a serious way.

They were held in the autumn only, after the maize-
10 *harvesting*, and below the full moon. These dances may have been a thousand years old. Some of them – which were highly approved of by the mothers and grandmothers of the dancers – were held by the white settlers to be *immoral*, and had them forbidden by law. Once,
15 when I came back from a holiday in Europe, I found that twenty-five of my young warriors had, in the middle of the coffee-picking season, been sent to prison for having danced a forbidden dance at a night Ngoma on the farm. My manager informed me that his wife could
20 not possibly put up with the dance. I was angry with the elders of the squatters for having held their Ngoma near my manager's house, but they explained to me that they had been dancing at Kathegu's **manyatta***, four or five miles away from it. I then had to go to Nairobi to talk
25 matters over with our D.C., who let the whole lot of dancers come back to the farm to pick coffee.

The night dances were fine shows. Here you are not in doubt as to the theatre of the show; it was formed by the fires and extended as far out as the light spread,

harvest, to cut and gather, here, the maize
immoral, not moral
*a group of huts

80

indeed fire was the central principle of the Ngoma. It was not really needed for the dancing, for the moon-light of the African highlands is wonderfully clear and white; it was brought to create an effect. The fire made a stage of the first order, it collected all the colours and movements within it into a unity. 5

Firewood was carried to the dancing place during the day before the dance by the squatter women and placed in the centre of the dancing ring. At night the old women took their seats round this centre, and from there a row of small fires, like a circle of stars, were fed 10 through the hours of the night. The dancers were run-ning and dancing outside the fires with the forest night as a background.

The guests arrived in small parties. Many of the dancers had walked fifteen miles to get to the Ngoma. 15 They brought flutes or drums with them, so that, on the night of the big dance, all the roads and pathways of the country would ring with music.

A dramatic *incident* took place at one of the night Ngomas. 20

The Ngoma was given in my honour a short time before I was going to Europe on a visit. We had had a good year: it was held in a great style, there may have been fifteen hundred Kikuyu present. The dance had 25 been going on for a few hours when, all at once, a movement ran through the ring of dancers, of surprise or fear, a strange sound, as when the wind blows through dry grass. The dance slowed down. I asked one of the old men what was the matter. He answered 30

incident, an event or a happening

81

quickly, in a low voice: "**Masai na-kudja**," – the Masai are coming.

It was against the law for the Masai to come to a Kikuyu Ngoma, too much trouble had come from this in the past. My houseboys came up and stood by my chair; everybody looked towards the entrance of the dancing ground. When the Masai came in, the dance stopped altogether.

There were twelve young Masai warriors walking in, and when they had taken a few steps they stopped, waited, and looked neither right nor left. They were naked except for their weapons and their splendid head-dresses. One of them wore the lion-skin head-dress of the Moran at war. It was felt that they had come to the Ngoma against their own will. The beating of the drum had run across the river into the reserve, had gone on and on, and troubled the hearts of the young warriors there; twelve of them had given in to the call.

The Kikuyu behaved well to their guests. The chief dancer of the farm welcomed them into the dancing ring, where in deep silence they took their place, and the dance was begun once more. It was, however, different from what it had been before. The drums began to beat in a louder voice, and a quicker *rhythm*. Had the Ngoma gone on, we should have seen how Kikuyu and Masai would have taken upon themselves to show one another their skill as dancers. But it did not come to that: there are things which cannot be carried through even with the good will of everybody concerned.

What happened I do not know. All of a sudden the

rhythm, a strong regular repeated pattern of sounds or movements

82

ring was broken, someone cried out loud; in a few seconds the whole place before me was a mass of running people, there was the sound of blows and of bodies falling to the ground, and over our heads the night air was filled with flying spears. We all got up to see what 5 was going on.

When the *emotions* had calmed down, a little space had cleared around me. Two of the old squatters came up to me and explained what had happened: how the Masai had started the trouble, and the present state of 10 things: a Masai and three Kikuyu wounded, "cut to pieces", their expression was. Would I now, please, *sew* them up again? Otherwise everybody was likely to get much trouble from the **Selikali** – the Government. I asked the old man what the fighters had had cut off. 15 "The head," he answered proudly. At that moment Kamante came across the place, carrying a *threaded needle* and my *thimble*. At the same time old Awaru came forward. He had learned to sew during the seven years

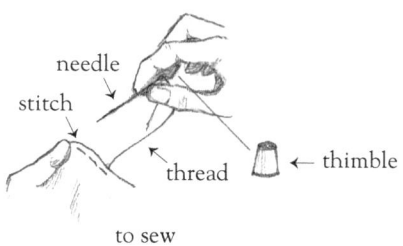

he had been in prison. He must have been looking for 20 an opportunity to show his abilities, for he immediate-

| *emotion*, a strong feeling

ly said he would take charge of the case. He did indeed
sew up the wounded, they got well under his hands, and
he himself, later, made much of his results. But
Kamante told me in confidence that the heads had not
been off.

As the presence of the Masai had been against the
law, we had to hide the wounded Masai in a hut. As
soon as he was well again, he disappeared without a
word of thanks to Awaru. It was hard, I believe, for the
heart of a Masai to be wounded – and healed – by
Kikuyu.

The *Noble* Pioneer

The visits of my friends to the farm were happy events.

When one of Denys Finch-Hatton's long safaris was
drawing to its end, it happened that I would find, on a
morning, a young Masai standing outside my house.
"Bwana is on his way back," he announced. "He will be
here in two or three days."

The great wanderers among my friends were pleased
to find that the farm remained the same whenever they
came to it. They had been over vast countries. They
had raised their *tents* in many places and they liked to
be met by familiar faces, and I had the same servants all
the time that I was in Africa.

As far as Berkeley Cole and Denys Finch-Hatton
were concerned, they considered everything in my

---

noble, having fine personal qualities; having a high social position,
especially by birth

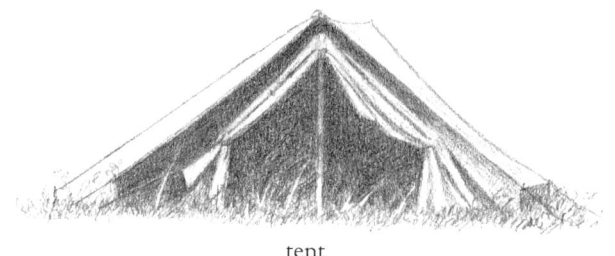

tent

house theirs, and brought the things they felt to be lacking. They brought books and *gramophone records* out from Europe for me.

Denys was a fine sportsman, a lover of music and art, but he should have been set in an earlier English land- 5 scape, in the days of Queen Elizabeth. He could indeed have been placed well in any period of our civilization up to the opening of the nineteenth century. He did cut a figure in his own age, but it did not quite fit in any- where. His friends in England always wanted him to 10 come back, they wrote out plans for a career for him there, but Africa was keeping him.

← gramophone
record

It was a sad thing that Jama, Berkeley's young Somali servant, was of a tribe at war with Farah's tribe. They exchanged dark deep glances over our dinner table when they were waiting on Berkeley and me. Late in
5 the evening we talked about what we would do if we came out in the morning and found both Farah and Jama cold, with knives in their hearts.

Berkeley, like his brother, Galbraith Cole, and his brother-in-law, Lord Delamere, was an early settler, a
10 pioneer of the colony, and *intimate* with the Masai, who in those days were the most important nation of the land. He had known them before the European civilization – which in the depths of their hearts they hated more than anything else in the world – had cut
15 through their roots; before they were moved from their beautiful north country. He could speak with them of the old days in their own language. Whenever Berkeley was staying on the farm, the Masai came over the river to see him. The old chiefs sat and discussed their
20 present troubles with him, his jokes would make them laugh, and it was as if a hard stone had laughed.

When the Great War* broke out, and the Masai had news of it, the blood of the old fighting tribe was up. I happened to be out, during the first months of the war,
25 alone with Natives and Somali, with three ox-wagons, doing transport for the English Government, and going through the Masai Reserve. Whenever the people of a new district heard of my arrival they came to my camp, with shining eyes, to ask me a hundred questions about
30 the war and the Germans – was it true that they were coming from the air? At night the young warriors came

intimate, having a close and friendly relationship
*World War I

86

to my tent in full war paint. They did not doubt then that they would be allowed to fight.

But the English Government did not want to organize the Masai to make war on white men, even Germans, and it forbade the Masai to fight, and put an end 5 to all their hopes. The Kikuyu were to take part in the war as carriers, but the Masai were to keep their hands off their weapons. But in 1918, when *conscription* had been introduced in regard to all the other Natives of the colony, the government thought it necessary to 10 call out the Masai as well. By this time the Masai had lost sympathy with the war and refused to come. The Morani of the district disappeared into the woods and the bush.

During the war, some of the old big Masai chiefs had, 15 however, made themselves useful to the English military by sending out their young men to *scout* on the movements of the Germans in the Reserve and on the border. When the war was over, the government wanted to thank them for their services. A number of *medals* 20 were sent out to be distributed among the Masai, and as

medal

conscription, the act of forcing somebody by law to serve in the armed forces
scout, to look in various places to find somebody or something

far as twelve of the medals were concerned Berkeley, who knew the Masai so well and could speak Masai, was asked to hand them out.

My farm bordered on the Masai Reserve and Berke-
5 ley came to ask me if he might stay with me and give out the medals from my house. On a Sunday we drove together a long way down into the Reserve and invited the chiefs in question to come to the farm on such and such a day.

10 The distribution of the medals, although in itself of no importance, was a great event. The old Masai had arrived, followed by their sons. They sat and waited on the lawn, from time to time discussing my cows there; perhaps they hoped to be given one in return for their
15 services.

Berkeley had an armchair carried out on the lawn in front of the house. He then came out followed by Jama who was wearing a very fine Arabian waistcoat, which Berkeley had let him buy for the occasion, and who
20 carried the box with the medals.

Berkeley stood up to speak, and he so impressed the old people that, one by one, they got to their feet, and stood facing him, their eyes on his. What the speech was about I cannot say, as it was in Masai. It sounded as
25 if he were informing them that an unbelievable *benefit* was given them because of their splendid behaviour. But seeing that it was Berkeley who spoke, and that from the faces of the Masai you would never learn anything, it may have contained something quite different.
30 When he had spoken, without a moment's pause he

benefit, a thing that one gains from

let Jama bring the box and took out the medals, *solemnly* reading out, one after another, the names of the Masai chiefs, and handing them the medals with an outstretched hand. The Masai took them from him silently. 5

A medal is not a practical thing to give to a naked man, because he has no place to fix it, and the old Masai chiefs kept standing with theirs in their hand. After a time a very old man came up to me, held out his hand with a medal in it, and asked me to tell him 10 what it had got on it. I explained it to him as well as I could. On the one side it had a head of Britannia*, and upon the other side the words: 'The Great War for Civilization'.

When Berkeley died, the country changed. His friends 15 felt it at the time and were very sad, and many people came to feel it later. An *epoch* in the history of the colony came to an end with him. Until his death the country had been the Happy Hunting Grounds, now it was slowly changing and turning into a business *propo-* 20 *sition.*

---

solemn, very serious and formal
*the figure of a seated woman, used as a symbol of the British Empire
epoch, a period of time marked by important events or special charac-
teristics
proposition, that which is offered for consideration

Wings

Denys Finch-Hatton had no other home in Africa than the farm. He lived in my house between his safaris, and
5 kept his books and his gramophone there. When he came to the farm, it gave out what was in it; it spoke – as the coffee-plantations speak, when they flower with the first showers of the rainy season. When I was expecting Denys back, and heard his car coming up the
10 drive, I heard, at the same time, the things on the farm telling me what they really were. He was happy on the farm; he came there only when he wanted to come. He never did but what he wanted to do, always true to himself and others.
15 Denys liked to hear a story told. Fashions have changed, and the art of listening to a story has been lost in Europe. The Natives of Africa, who cannot read, have still got it; if you begin a story: "There was a man who walked out on the plain, and there he met anoth-
20 er man," you have them with you, their minds running along the unknown tracks of the men on the plain. But white people, even if they feel that they ought to, cannot listen to a story, they are unable to remain still and quiet, or they fall asleep. They will ask you for some-
25 thing to read.

Denys preferred listening to a story; when he came to the farm he would ask: "Have you got a story?" I had made up many while he had been away. In the evenings he made himself comfortable in front of the
30 fire, and with me sitting on the floor, cross-legged like Scheherazade* herself, he would listen, clear-eyed, to a

*the princess of 'The Arabian Nights' who told a thousand and one stories to save her life

90

long *tale*, from beginning to end. He kept better account of it than I did myself, and at the dramatic appearance of one of the characters, would stop me to say: "That man died at the beginning of the story, but never mind." 5

The gramophone he had given me brought new life to the farm, it became the voice of the farm. Sometimes Denys would arrive unexpectedly at the house, when I was out in the coffee-field, bringing new records with him. He would set the gramophone going, and as I 10 came riding back at sunset, the music streaming towards me in the clear *cool* air of the evening would announce his presence to me. The Natives liked the gramophone, and used to stand round the house to listen to it; some of my houseboys picked out a favourite 15 piece of music and asked me for it when I was alone with them in the house.

When we were together, Denys and I had great luck with lions. The Masai sometimes came to my house and asked me to come out and shoot a certain lion 20 which was killing off their cattle. Farah and I had been out walking in the early morning without as much as finding the tracks of a lion. But when Denys and I went for a ride, the lions would be about, we could come upon them then at a meal, or see them crossing the dry 25 river-beds.

One morning during the spring rains, Mr Nichols, a South African, who was then my manager, came to my house to tell me that in the night two lions had been

---

tale, story
cool, cold in a fresh and nice way

to the farm and had killed two of our oxen and dragged them into the coffee-plantation. One of them they had eaten up there, but the other was lying among the coffee-trees. If the lions were left in peace over this crime,
5 he said, they would come back another time. The oxen were our best working animals and we could not afford to lose any more. I said that the best thing would be to shoot them.

"And who is going to shoot them?" asked Nichols.
10 "I am a married man and I have no wish to risk my life unnecessarily." No, I said, I did not mean to make him shoot the lions. But Mr Finch-Hatton had arrived the night before, he and I would go.

I went in to find Denys and together we went down
15 and found the dead oxen in the coffee-plantation, as Nichols had told me; it had hardly been touched by the lions. The tracks were deep and clear in the soft ground, two big lions had been here in the night. They were easy to follow through the plantation and up to
20 the wood, but by the time we came there it had rained so heavily that it was difficult to see anything, and we lost the tracks in the grass and the bush at the edge of the wood.

Denys had great experience with lions. He said that
25 they would come back early in the night to finish the meal, and that we ought to give them time to settle down to it, and go down to the field ourselves at nine o'clock. We would have to take an electric *torch*, that Denys had with him on his safaris, to shoot by. He

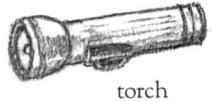

torch

92

made me choose who should hold the torch and who should shoot, and I said that I would hold the torch for him.

We had dinner and at nine o'clock we went out.

It was raining a little, but there was a moon; from 5 time to time she put out her white face high up in the sky, behind the thin clouds, shining on the white-flowering coffee-field. We passed the school at a distance; it was all lit up. At this sight I felt great pride in my people. Here were two lions just outside their door, but 10 my children had not let the lions keep them away from school.

We walked silently between two rows of coffee-trees not far from where the dead ox was lying. I began to shake with *excitement*. I was afraid to get too near to 15 Denys for fear that he might feel it and send me back, but I could not keep too far away from him either, for he might need my torchlight any moment.

The lions, we found afterwards, had been on the kill. When they heard us or smelt us, they had walked off a 20 little way into the coffee-field to let us pass. Probably because they thought that we were passing too slowly, one of them gave a low *growl*, in front and to the right of us. It was so low that we were not even sure that we had heard it. Denys stopped a second; without turning 25 he asked me: "Did you hear?" "Yes," I said.

We walked a little further and the deep growling was repeated, this time straight to the right. "Put on the light," Denys said. It was not altogether an easy job, for

excitement, a strong feeling one has when one is both eager and nervous
growl, (of animals) to make a low threatening sound

93

he was much taller than me, and I had to get the light over his shoulder onto his rifle and beyond. As I lit the torch the whole world changed, the wet leaves on the coffee-trees shone, and the tracks on the ground
5 showed up quite clearly.

I moved the circle of light on, and there was the lion. He stood facing us, and he looked very light against the black African night behind him. The shot was fired, close to me, and the lion went down like a
10 stone. "Move on, move on," Denys cried to me. I turned the torch, but my hand was shaking so badly that the circle of light, which held all the world, and which I commanded, danced around. I heard Denys laugh beside me in the dark. - "The torch-work on the
15 second lion," he said to me later, "was a little shaky." – But in the centre of the dance was the second lion, moving away from us and half hidden by a coffee-tree. As the light reached him he turned his head and Denys shot. He fell out of the circle, but got up and into it
20 again, he swung round towards us, and just as the second shot was fired, he gave one long, angry growl.

Africa, in a second, grew endlessly big, and Denys and I, standing upon it, so very small. Outside our torchlight there was nothing but darkness, in the dark-
25 ness in two directions there were lions, two big dead animals, and from the sky rain, and the silence of the night all round.

By now all the children were coming out of the school, running down the road. They stopped where
30 we could see them and cried out in a low, soft voice: "Msabu. Are you there? Are you there? Msabu, Msabu."

I sat on a lion and cried back to them: "Yes, I am."

"Has Bwana shot the lions? Both of them?" They were all over the place at once, jumping up and down, making a song about the event; it ran as follows: "Three shots. Two lions. Three shots. Two lions. Three good shots, two big bad kali lions." 5

In a short time a great number of people came to the spot, carrying hurricane lamps. They stood round the lions and talked about them, and Kanuthia, who had brought knives, started to skin them. With all this the coffee-field became very lively, the rain stopped, the 10 moon shone down on them all.

We went back to the house and Juma opened a bottle of wine. We were too wet, and too dirty with mud and blood to sit down to it, but stood up before the fire in the dining-room and drank our wine up quickly. We 15 did not say a word. In our hunt we had been one unit and we had nothing to say to one another.

To Denys Finch-Hatton I *owe* what was, I think, the greatest pleasure of my life on the farm: I flew with him over Africa. There, where there are few or no roads and where you can land on the plains, flying becomes a
5 thing of real and vital importance in your life, it opens up a world. Denys had brought out his Moth machine; it could land on the plain on my farm only a few minutes from the house, and we were up nearly every day.

You have tremendous views as you get up above the
10 African highlands, surprising combinations and changes of light and colouring. The language is short of words for the experiences of flying. When you have flown over the Rift Valley you have travelled far and have been to the lands on the other side of the moon.
15 You may at other times fly low enough to see the animals on the plains and to feel towards them as God did when he had just created them.

4. *FAREWELL* TO THE FARM

Hard Times

My farm was a little too high up for growing coffee. In the cold months we would get *frost* and in the mornings
20 the young coffee-berries would be withered. The wind

owe something to somebody, to recognize somebody as the cause or source of something
farewell, goodbye
frost, a weather condition when the temperature falls below zero

blew in from the plains, and even in good years we never got the same amount of coffee to the acre as the people in the lower districts of Thika and Kiambu, at four thousand feet.

We were short of rain, as well, in the Ngong country, 5 and three times we had a year of real drought. On parts of the farm we also got bad coffee diseases.

At the same time coffee prices fell. We could not pay our debts, and we had no money to run the plantation. My people at home, who had put money into the farm, 10 wrote to me and told me that I would have to sell.

I thought of many ways of saving the farm. One year I tried to grow *flax* on our spare land. It is a lovely job, but it needs much skill and experience which the Kikuyu could not be taught in the turn of a hand; so my 15 flax-growing was no success. I did not have any luck with my other experiments.

If I had had the capital I would have given up coffee and planted forest trees on my land. Trees grow so quickly in Africa, in ten years' time you walk under 20 them. I would have had a good market for both *timber* and firewood in Nairobi. The squatters kept on looking forward hopefully to the time when everybody would have lots of firewood – such as the people had had in the old days – from the forest that I was now soon going 25 to plant.

Two years before I left Africa I was in Europe on a visit. I travelled back in the coffee-picking season, so that I could not get news of the harvest before I came

flax, a small plant used for making sheets among many other household things
timber, wood prepared for use in building

to Mombasa. All the time on the boat, the problem was on my mind.

Farah came to meet me in Mombasa. I was afraid to mention the coffee harvest right way. We talked of oth-
5 er news of the farm for some time. Then I could not put it off any longer and I asked him how many tons of cof-fee they had picked. The Somali are generally pleased to announce a disaster. But here Farah was not happy; he was extremely grave. He half closed his eyes and laid
10 back his head. He was very sad when he said: "Forty tons, Memsahib." At that I knew I could not carry on. All colour and life faded out of the world round me. I did not say anything more to Farah, and he did not speak again, but walked away, the last friendly being in
15 my world.

The same year the grasshoppers came on the land. It was said that they came from Abyssinia; after two years of drought up there, they travelled south and ate up all *vegetation* on their way. Up north the land was one vast
20 desert where they had passed. The settlers sent runners to their neighbours to the south to announce the com-ing of the grasshoppers. Still you could not do much against them even if you were warned. On all the farms people had had firewood and maize-*stalks* ready and set
25 fire to them when the grasshoppers came, and they sent out all the farm labourers with empty *tins*, and told them to shout and beat the tins to stop them landing. But it did not last long, for however much the farmers

tin

vegetation, plants in general
stalk, see picture, page 6

98

would frighten them, the grasshoppers could not keep up in the air for ever; the only thing that each farmer could hope for was to drive them off to the next farm to the south, and the more farms they were driven away from, the hungrier they were when finally they settled. 5

One afternoon when I was out riding I saw a few grasshoppers on the path. I passed my manager's house and told him to have everything ready to receive the grasshoppers. As together we were looking north we saw a shadow on the sky like a long stretch of black 10 smoke. From time to time a grasshopper *swished* past us in the air, or dropped on the ground.

The next morning as I opened my door and looked out, the whole landscape outside was a pale reddish-brown colour. The trees, the lawn, the drive, all that I 15 could see was covered with that colour. The grasshoppers were sitting there. While I was looking at them, they moved and lifted, after a few minutes the atmosphere *fluttered* with wings, they were leaving.

That time they did not do much damage to the farm, 20 they had been staying with us overnight only. They had broken a couple of big trees in my drive simply by sitting on them, and when you looked at the trees and remembered that each of the grasshoppers is only about an inch and a half long, you began to get an idea of the 25 number of them.

The grasshoppers came again; for two or three months we had continued attacks of them. We soon gave up trying to frighten them off, it was a hopeless task. When the flight was at its highest it was like a 30

swish, to move with a soft sound
flutter, to move lightly and quickly

strong wind, little thin wings, hard as steel to all sides of you and over your head, shining in the sun, but themselves darkening the sun. They flutter against your face, get inside your clothes and shoes. They fill you with a sickening *rage* and despair. The individual among the mass does not count, kill it and it makes no difference.

They never did much harm to the coffee-plantation; the leaves of the coffee-trees are too hard for them to eat. But the maize-fields were a sad sight after they had been there, and there was nothing left of my garden. The shambas of the squatters were like stretches of cleared and burnt land.

When I had no more money, I had to sell the farm. A big company in Nairobi bought it. They meant to take up all the coffee-trees, to divide up the land and lay out roads, and in time, when Nairobi would be growing out to the west, they meant to sell the land for building *plots*.

I was to remain on the farm, in charge of it, until after the coffee harvest, and things were to go on as before. During this time, I thought, something would happen to change it all back.

In this way began a strange period in my existence. The truth that the farm was no longer mine, could simply be ignored. It made no difference to things in my day-to-day life. It was then, from hour to hour, a lesson in the art of living in the moment, or, it might be said, in *eternity*, in which the actual happenings of the

rage, uncontrolled anger
plot, a small piece of land intended for a special purpose
eternity, time without end

moment make but little difference.

I did not, during this time, ever believe that I would have to give up the farm or to leave Africa. I was told that I must do so by the people around me. I had letters from home by each mail to prove it, and all the facts of my daily life pointed to it. All the same I kept on believing that I would spend the rest of my life in Africa. I simply could not imagine anything else.

The Natives on the farm looked to me for help and support, and did not attempt to arrange their future for themselves. They tried their very best to make me stay on, and for this purpose they had many plans which they told me. At the time when the sale of the farm was through, they came and sat round my house from early morning till night, not so much in order to talk with me as just to follow all my movements. The Kikuyu took the situation better than I did, on account of their greater inside knowledge of God and the Devil.

Their presence made me feel good. The understanding between us lay deeper than all reason. In the night, I counted the hours till the time when the Kikuyu should turn up again at my house.

The Death of Kinanjui

In that same year the Chief Kinanjui died. One of his sons came to my house late in the evening and asked me to go back with him to his father's village, for he was dying: Na-taka kufa – he wants to die – the Natives have it.

Kinanjui was now an old man. A great thing had lately happened in his life: the quarantine regulations

of the Masai Reserve had been *suspended*. As soon as he heard it, the old Kikuyu chief went south into the Reserve with a few servants to finish his accounts with the Masai and bring back the cows that belonged to
5 him. While he was down there he had fallen ill. His men had done their best for him and had taken great trouble to get him home. Now he lay dying in his hut, and had sent for me.

Kinanjui's son had come to my house after dinner,
10 and it was dark when Farah and I and he drove over to his village, but the moon was up and in her first quarter. On the way Farah opened up the subject of who was to *succeed* Kinanjui as chief of the Kikuyu. The old Chief had many sons; it appeared that there were var-
15 ious influences at work in the Kikuyu world. Two of his sons were Christians, but one was a Roman Catholic, and the other had converted to the Church of Scotland. Each of the two missions was sure to take pains to get their favourite to succeed Kinanjui. The Kikuyu
20 themselves, it seemed, wanted a third, younger son who was not a Christian.

Kinanjui's big manyatta was all quiet under the moon. It looked dark, but was not asleep. People were up and came and surrounded us when they heard the
25 car. A boy with a lamp came along and took us to Kinanjui's hut, and a crowd of people went with us and stood outside it.

Inside two fires were burning on the floor, the heat was terrible and the smoke so thick that at first I could
30 not see who was in there, although they had a hurri-

---

suspend, to stop something for a time
succeed, to come next after somebody and take their place

cane lamp standing on the floor. When I had got used
to the atmosphere I saw that there were three old men,
a very old woman, a young, pretty girl and a young boy
in the hut. Kinanjui was lying flat on his bed, dying,
and the *stench* was so bad that at first I was afraid to
open my mouth to speak for fear that I should be sick.

Kinanjui's son brought in an old European chair,
with one leg shorter that the others, and placed it very
close to the bed, for me to sit on. Kinanjui could still
see, and when I came up to the bed he turned his eyes
on me and kept them on my face all the time that I was
in the hut.

Very slowly he dragged his right hand across his body
to touch my hand. He was in terrible pain, but he was
still himself and lay with great dignity naked on his
bed. The boy, whom I took to be a late-born son of
Kinanjui's, came up close to his father's bed and told
me what they had agreed on before I arrived.

The doctor from the mission, he explained, had
heard of Kinanjui's illness and had been to see him. He
had told the Kikuyu that he would come back again to
take the dying chief into the mission hospital that same
night. But Kinanjui did not want to go to hospital.
That was why he had sent for me. He wanted me to
take him with me to my own house now, before the
people from the mission returned. While the boy
spoke, Kinanui looked at me.

I sat and listened with a heavy heart. A year ago or
even three months ago, I would have taken him with
me. But today was different. Things had gone badly for

stench, very bad smell

103

me lately and had made me fear that they would get worse. I had been spending days in the offices of Nairobi, listening to businessmen and lawyers. The house, to which Kinanjui asked me to take him, was no longer mine.

He was going to die, he could not be saved. He would die in my car on the way home and the mission people would say that it was my fault. All this, from my seat on the broken chair in the hut, seemed to me a weight too heavy to take on. I could no longer stand up against the authorities of the world. I would have to leave him.

I got up and went across the room to Farah and told him that I could not take Kinanjui with me. Farah's eyes and whole face darkened with surprise.

I went back to his bed and told him that I could not take him with me. There was no need to give reasons, so we left it at that. Kinanjui did not move or change in any way, he kept his eyes on me as he had done all the time.

"**Kwaheri**, Kinanjui," I said – Good-bye.

It was very cold outside. The moon was now low down at the horizon, it must have been past midnight.

Kinanjui died that same night, at the mission hospital. Two of his sons came over to my house the next afternoon to tell me. They asked me to the *funeral*, which was to take place on the following day, near his village, at Dagoretti.

The Kikuyu, when left to themselves, do not bury their dead, but leave them above ground for the hye-

funeral, the religious occasion when a dead person is *buried*, that is put in the ground (or burned)

104

nas and vultures to deal with. The custom had always appealed to me, I thought that it would be a pleasant thing to be laid out to the sun and the stars and be so quickly and openly picked and cleaned; to be made one with nature and become a common part of the 5 landscape. But the government had taken much trouble to make the Kikuyu change their ways, and to teach them to lay their dead in the ground, but they still did not like the idea at all.

Kinanjui, they now told me, was to be buried. Per- 10 haps the Kikuyu wanted to make a great Native show and gathering of the occasion. I drove over to Dagoretti, on the following afternoon, expecting to find all the minor chiefs of the country.

But Kinanjui's funeral was altogether a European 15 and church affair. There were a few government representatives present, the District Commissioner and two officials from Nairobi. The day and the place belonged to the church; the plain, in the sun, was black with them. Both the French Mission and the Missions of 20 the Church of England and Scotland were richly represented. If they wished to impress the Kikuyu with the feeling that here they had laid their hands on the dead chief, and that he now belonged to them, they were successful. They were so obviously in power that one 25 felt it to be out of the question for Kinanjui to get away from them. This is an old trick of the Church's. Here I saw the mission-boys, the converted Natives, fat young Kikuyu with glasses and *folded hands*. Probably Kinanjui's two Christian sons were there, but I did not know 30

to fold one's hands, to bring or hold one's hands together

105

them. Some of the old chiefs were attending the funeral, but they kept themselves in the background.

In the end Kinanjui was put in the ground of his own country, and covered with it. When Farah and I drove back he was very silent. For two days he had been like a lost soul because I had not wanted to take Kinanjui back to my house with me.

As we drove up before the door he said: "Never mind, Memsahib."

The *Grave* in the Hills

Denys Finch-Hatton had come in from one of his safaris, and he had stayed for a little while on the farm, but, when I began to break up my house and to pack, and he could stay there no longer, he went away and lived in Hugh Martin's house in Nairobi. From there he drove out to the farm every day.

Most of the time we talked and acted as if the future did not exist; it had never been his way to worry about it, for it was as if he knew that he could draw on forces unknown to us if he wanted to.

He talked of packing up his books that had been in my house for many years, but he never got any further with the job.

grave, a hole made in the ground for a dead body; the earth or stone placed over this

106

"You keep them," he said, "now I have no place to put them."

Denys owned a piece of land down by the coast, thirty miles north of Mombasa on the Creek of Takaunga. Here were the ruins of an old Arab settlement with a small minaret. He had built a small house on his land and I had stayed there. The place was beautiful with the blue Indian Ocean before you as far as the eye reached.

Denys sometimes talked of making Takaunga his home in Africa, and of starting his safaris from there. When I began to talk of having to leave the farm, he offered me his house down there, as he had had mine in the highlands. But Takaunga was too low and too hot for me.

In the month of May of the year I left Africa, Denys went down there for a week. He was planning to build a larger house. He went away in his aeroplane, intending to make his way home around by Voi to see if there were any elephants there for his safaris.

Denys was subject to special kinds of *moods*, and under their influence at times he became silent for days, though he did not know of it himself and was surprised when I asked him what was the matter with him. The last days before he started on this journey to the coast, he was in this manner *absent-minded*, but when I spoke of it he laughed at me.

I asked him to let me come with him. First he said yes, and then he changed his mind. He could not take me; the journey round Voi was going to be very rough,

---

mood, the state of one's feelings or mind at a particular time
absent-minded, showing that one is not really thinking about what is being said or done around one

he might have to land and to sleep in the bush, so that it would be necessary for him to take a Native boy with him. This was the only time that I asked Denys to take me with him on his aeroplane that he would not do it.

5   He went off on Friday the eighth. "Look out for me on Thursday," he said when he went, "I shall be back in time to have lunch with you." Then he drove away, waving to me.

When Denys was down in Mombasa, he broke a *pro-*
10 *peller* while landing. He asked the East Africa Airway Company to send some spare parts and they sent a boy to Mombasa with them. When the aeroplane was fixed, and Denys was going up again, he told the Airways boy to come with him. But the boy would not come. This
15 boy was used to flying, and had been up with many people, and with Denys, too. But this time the boy would not go up with him.

propeller

A long time after, when he met Farah in Nairobi, he said to Farah: "Not for a hundred rupees would I, then,
20 have gone up with Bwana Bedâr." The shadow of destiny, which Denys himself had felt the last days at Ngong, was seen more strongly by the Native.

So Denys took Kamau, his own boy, with him to Voi. Poor Kamau was afraid of flying. He had told me that when he got up and away from the ground, he fixed his eyes on his feet and kept them there till he got down to earth again.

I looked out for Denys on Thursday. But when he did not come, I drove to Nairobi as I had things to do there. Here a strange mood stole upon me and grew so strong that I wondered if I were beginning to go mad. The town seemed very sad, and people I met turned away from me: my friends, when they saw me, got into their cars and drove away. I was to lunch with Lady McMillan at Chiromo*, and I thought that there I should find people to talking to, and get back my balance.

But it was the same thing at Chiromo as in the streets of Nairobi. Everybody seemed very sad, and as I came in the talking stopped. I sat beside my old friend Mr Bulpett, and he looked down and said only a few words. I thought: These people are no good to me, I will go back to the farm, Denys will be there by now.

But when we had finished lunch, Lady McMillan asked me to come with her into her small sitting-room, and there told me that there had been an accident at Voi. Denys's machine had fallen down and he had been killed.

It was then as I had thought: at the sound of Denys's name even, the truth was revealed, and I knew and understood everything.

I remembered how Denys had told me that he wished to be buried in the Ngong Hills. I had not remembered it until now, it had been so far from my thoughts that they should mean to bury him at all. Now it was as if a picture had been shown to me.

*name of a restaurant

There was a place in the hills in the Game Reserve that I myself, at the time when I thought that I was to live and die in Africa, had pointed out to Denys as my future grave. In the evening, while we sat looking at
5 the hills from my house, he remarked that then he would like to be buried there himself as well. Since then, when we drove out in the hills, Denys said: "Let us drive as far as our graves."

My Norwegian friend, Gustav Mohr, had come from
10 his farm to my house, when he heard of Denys's death. Hugh Martin came, too, and I told them of Denys's wish. They told the people at Voi who informed me that they would bring Denys's body up by train the next morning, so that the funeral could take place in the
15 hills at noon. I must have his grave ready by then.

It rained all night, and there was a fine drizzling rain in the morning when I and Gustav Mohr left. Driving up in the hills was like driving into the clouds. We could not see the plains below to our left, nor the peaks
20 of the hills to our right. The mist grew thicker the higher we came up. We found the place where we could come into the Game Reserve, so we drove on a few hundred yards and then got out of the car. The morning air was so cold that it bit the fingers.

25 We had been walking about in the mist for an hour, so we had to decide where the grave should be now, or we would not have it ready in time.

"I cannot see where we are," I said, "let us wait a little longer."

30 We waited in silence in the long grass while I smoked a cigarette. Then the mist spread a little and after ten minutes we could see where we were. The plains lay below us, and I could follow the road by

which we had come. To the south far away below the changing clouds, lay the broken, dark blue foothills of Kilimanjaro. Suddenly, much closer, to the east below us, was a little red spot in the grey and green, the roof of my house on its cleared place in the forest. We did not have to go any further, we were in the right place.

There was a narrow, natural terrace in the hillside. Here we marked out the place for the grave. We called up the boys, and told them to cut the grass and *dig* the grave.

Some cars came out from Nairobi, and we sent down a boy to show them the way. The Somali of Nairobi came. Some of Denys's friends from up-country, who had heard the news of his death, came driving from Naivasha, Gil-Gil, and Elmenteita. Now the day grew clearer, and the four tall peaks of the hills showed above us against the sky.

Here in the early afternoon they brought Denys from Nairobi, following his old safari track to Tanganyika, and driving slowly on the wet road. They carried the narrow *coffin* up to the grave and placed it in it. The hills stood up gravely, they knew and understood what we were doing there. It was an action between them and him, and the people present became a party of very small lookers-on in the landscape.

In the days after Denys's death, his safari servants gathered on the farm. They did not ask for anything, but sat down with their backs to the wall, most of the time in

---

dig, to make a hole by breaking up and moving the earth
coffin, box in which a dead person is buried

111

silence. Bilea Isa, Denys's Somali servant, came down
from Naivasha to the farm. Bilea had been to England
twice with Denys, had been to school there, and spoke
English like a gentleman. Some years ago, Denys and I
5 had attended Bilea's wedding in Nairobi; the feast last-
ed for seven days. Bilea came down to see his master's
grave and sit on it.

Farah went out and talked to them. He, too, was
very grave. "It would not have been so bad," he said to
10 me, "that you were leaving the country, if only Bedâr
had still been here."

Denys's boys stayed for about a week, then they left,
one after the other.

I often drove out to Denys's grave. In a straight line,
15 it was not more than five miles from my house, but
round by the road it was fifteen. The grave was a thousand feet higher up than my house, the air was different here, as clear as a glass of water; light sweet winds
lifted your hair when you took off your hat. Over the
20 peaks of the hills, the clouds came wandering from the
east, drew their live shadow over the wide hilly land,
and disappeared over the Rift Valley.

Later on, Denys's brother, Lord Winchilsea, had a
stone set on his grave. In England his old school-fel-
25 lows, in memory of him, built a stone bridge over a
small stream between two fields at Eton. They put his
name on it, and the dates of his stay at Eton, and the
words: "Famous in these fields and by his many friends
much beloved."

30 After I had left Africa, Gustav Mohr wrote to me of
a strange thing that had happened by Denys's grave.
"The Masai," he wrote, "have reported to the District
Commissioner at Ngong, that many times, at sunrise

112

and sunset, they have seen lions on Finch-Hatton's grave in the Hills."

Farah and I Sell Out

Now I was alone on the farm. It was no longer mine, but the people who had bought it, had offered to let me stay in the house as long as I liked.   5

I was selling my furniture, which gave Farah and me a good deal to do. I packed my books in cases and sat on them, or had dinner on them. In the end there were no things in the rooms at all, and to my mind at the time they seemed, in this state, more fit to live in than 10 they had before.

Farah understood me very well. During this time he was concentrating on helping me in everything. He wore his best clothes every day. He had a lot of fine clothes: gold-*embroidered* Arab waistcoats, that I had 15 given him, and silk turbans in beautiful colours. Normally, he only wore them on special occasions, but now he put on the best he had. He walked one step behind me in the streets of Nairobi, or waited on the dirty stairs in the government buildings and lawyers' offices, 20 dressed like a prince. It took a Somali to do that.

The fate of my squatters was on my mind. As the people who had bought the farm were planning to dig up the coffee-trees, and to have the land cut up and sold

---

embroider, here, to make the waistcoat beatiful by sewing patterns onto it with gold thread

113

as building plots, they had no use for the squatters, and had given them six months' notice to get off the farm. They had never expected this, for they had lived in the *illusion* that the land was theirs. Many of them had been born on the farm, and others had come there as small children with their fathers.

The squatters knew that in order to stay on the land they had to work for me one hundred and eighty days out of each year, for which they were paid twelve shillings for every thirty days; these accounts were kept at the farm office. They also knew that they must pay the hut-tax to the government. My squatters had, from time to time, been threatened to be turned off the farm for an offence, so they must in some way have felt that their position could be questioned. For some time they chose to ignore the decision of the new owners.

In the end, the certainty of their notice to leave brought the squatters in dark groups to my house. They felt it was the consequence of my *departure* from the farm – my own bad luck was growing, and was spreading over them as well. They did not say that it was my fault, for that was talked out between us; they asked me where they were to go.

I found it difficult to answer them. The Natives cannot, according to the law, buy any land themselves, and there was no other farm that I knew of that was big enough to take them on as squatters. I told them they must go into the Kikuyu Reserve and find land there. They gravely asked me if they would find enough unoccupied land in the Reserve to bring all their cattle with them. And, they went on, would they all be sure to find

illusion, false idea, belief or impression
departure, the act of going away

114

land in the same place, so that the people from the farm could remain together, for they did not want to be separated.

I was surprised to find them so determined to stay together, for on the farm they had found it difficult to keep peace, and had never had much good to say of one another. Still, here they all came, the big cattle-owners like Kathegu, Kaninu, and Mauge, hand in hand, so to say, with the simple workers of the soil like Waweru and Chotha, who did not own so much as one goat; and they were all filled with one spirit, and as determined to keep one another as to keep their cows. I felt that they were not only asking me for a place to live, but that they were demanding their existence of me.

It is more than their land that you take away from the people, whose native land you take. It is their past as well, their roots and their identity. If you take away the things that they have been used to seeing, and will be expecting to see, you might as well take their eyes.

The Masai, when they were moved from their old country to the present Masai Reserve, took with them the names of their hills, plains, and rivers; and gave them to the hills, plains, and rivers of the new country. The Masai were carrying their cut roots with them as a medicine, and were trying, in exile, to hold on to their past in this way.

Now my squatters felt that if they were to go away from their land, they must have people round them who had known it, in order to keep their identity.

"Go, Msabu," they said to me, "go for us to the Selikali, and obtain permission from them that we may take all our cattle with us to the new place and that we shall remain together where we are going."

With this began for me a long *beggar's* journey which took up my last months in Africa.

First I went to the District Commissioners of Nairobi and Kiambu, then to the Native Department and the
5 Land Office, and finally to the *Governor*, Sir Joseph Byrne. In the end I forgot what I went for. Sometimes I had to stay in Nairobi for a whole day, or to go in two or three times a day.

The government officials were good people. The
10 difficulties were not of their making: it was really a problem to find an unoccupied stretch of land big enough to take in the full number of the people and their cattle, in the Kikuyu Reserve.

Most of the officials had been in the country for a
15 long time, and knew the Natives well. They knew that they would not sell any of their stock, and by bringing their herds to a place that was too small for them, they would cause, in years to come, endless trouble with their neighbours in the Reserve.

20 But when we came to the second request, that they should remain together, the people in authority said that there was no real need for that. In the end, just as I was beginning to feel that I must drive to Nairobi and back, and talk on in government offices all my life, I
25 was suddenly informed that my application had been granted. The government had agreed to give a piece of the Dagoretti Forest Reserve to the squatters of my farm. Here they could form a settlement of their own, not far from their old place, and they could still keep
30 their faces and their names, as a community.

beggar, a person who is asking for help, especially money
governor, a person appointed to govern, this is to rule, a province or state, especially a colony abroad

116

The news was received on the farm with deep silent emotion. They still stayed on, watching me in a new way. Natives have such faith in fortune that now, after our one success, they may have begun to trust that all was going to be well, and that I was to stay on the farm. 5

After two or three days, the feeling came upon me that my work in the country had been brought to an end, and that now I might go. The coffee harvest was finished, the house was empty, the squatters had got their land. The rains were over, and the new grass was 10 already long on the plains and in the hills.

Farewell

At that time the old men of the neighbourhood decided to hold a special Ngoma for me.

These Ngomas of the Ancients had been great events in the past, but now they were rarely danced, 15 and during all my time in Africa I had never seen one of them. I should have liked to do so, for the Kikuyu themselves thought highly of them. It was considered an honour to the farm that the old men's dance was to be performed there; my people talked of it a long time 20 before it was to take place.

Even Farah, who generally looked down on the Native Ngomas, was impressed this time. "These people are very old, Memsahib," he said, "very, very old."

There was one thing about these Ngomas which I 25 did not know - that they were forbidden by the government. The Kikuyu must have known that, but they probably reasoned that in these great troubled times, things might be done that in ordinary times could not be done, or else they had forgotten about it in the middle of the strong emotions set going by the dance. They did not even keep silent about it.

When the old dancers arrived they were a rare *sublime* sight.

There were about a hundred of them, naked, their warpaint *discreetly* put on. They did not try to obtain a youthful appearance; the whole point and weight of the dance lay in their old age.

As I stood looking at them, a feeling took hold of me that had taken hold of me before: It was not I who was going away, I did not have it in my power to leave Africa, but it was the country that was slowly and gravely withdrawing from me.

The old men did not speak, not even to one another, they were saving their strength for the coming effort.

Just as they had arranged themselves for the dance, an official from Nairobi arrived at the house with a letter for me, saying that the Ngoma must not take place. I did not understand it and I had to read the the paper through several times.

During all my years in Africa I have not lived through another moment of such *bitterness*. The old Kikuyu stood like a herd of old sheep, their eyes fixed upon my face. They could not, in a second, give up the thing on which their hearts had been set. Some of them made little movements with their legs; they had

---

sublime, of the best and most excellent kind
discreet, not too obvious
bitterness, a feeling of great anger or dislike because of something that one thinks is unfair

come to dance and dance they must. In the end I told them that our Ngoma was off.

The people of the farm who were most sad at my departure were, I think, the old women. The old Kikuyu women had a hard life. They were more diffi- 5 cult for any disease to kill off than their men, as I learned in my practice as a doctor. They had borne a number of children and had seen many of them die; they were afraid of nothing.

We had always been friends. They called me Jerie; 10 the men and the children – except the very young – never used the name for me. Jerie is a Kikuyu female name. It has a special quality. Whenever a girl is born a long time after her brothers and sisters, she is named Jerie, and I suppose that name has a note of affection 15 in it.

I keep a picture in my mind of a Kikuyu woman. I did not know her name, for I did not know her well. She came towards me on a path on the plain, carrying on her back a load of sticks which the Kikuyu use for con- 20 structing the roofs of their huts. This is women's work. The sticks may be fifteen feet long. These had been blackened by the smoke of the hut over many years. That meant that she had been pulling down her house and was carrying her building materials to new grounds. 25 When we met she stood dead still. After a moment tears began to stream down her face. Not a word did she or I speak, and after a few minutes we parted and walked on in opposite directions. I thought that after all she had some materials with which to begin her new 30 house, and I imagined how she would set to work, and tie her sticks together, and make herself a roof.

When in the end, the day came on which I was going away, I learned the strange lesson that things can happen which we cannot possibly imagine, either before, or at the time when they are taking place, or afterwards when we look back on them. Circumstances can have a force by which they bring about events without help of human imagination or understanding. On such occasions you keep in touch with what is going on by carefully following it from moment to moment, like a blind person who is being led. Things are happening to you, and you feel them happening, but except for this one fact, you have no connection with them, and no key to the cause or meaning of them. The performing wild animals in a circus go through their programme, I believe, in the same way. Those who have been through such an event can, in a way say that they have been through death – a passage outside the range of imagination, but within the range of experience.

Gustav Mohr came out in his car in the early morning to go to the railway station with me. It was a cool morning with but little colour in the air or the landscape. He, too, looked pale. We had tea together on the stone table outside the house, as we had had many times before. Here, to the west, the hills before us, in the grey mist, lived gravely through another moment of their many thousand years. I was very cold as if I had been up there.

My houseboys were still in the empty house, but they had, so to say, already moved to other quarters, their families and their belongings had been sent off. Farah's women had gone to the Somali village the day before.

Farah himself was going with me as far as Mombasa.

120

I said good-bye to each of my houseboys, and, as I went out, they, who had been told to close the doors, left the door wide open behind me, as if they thought that I was to come back again, or they did so to say that there was now nothing more to close the doors of the 5 house on, and they might as well be open to all winds. Farah drove me, slowly, at the pace of a riding-camel I suppose, round by the drive and out of sight of the house.

Many of my friends had come down to the station to 10 see me off. Hugh Martin was there and Lord Delamere, a little older, a little whiter. Most of the Somali of Nairobi were on the platform. The old cattle-trader Abdallah came up and gave me a ring to bring me luck. Bilea, Denys's servant, gravely asked me to give his 15 respects to his master's brother in England.

Gustav Mohr and I shook hands when I was already on the train. He wished so strongly to give me courage that his bright eyes shone and his face *flushed*.

At Samburu station, I got out of the train while the 20 engine was taking in water, and walked with Farah on the platform.

From there, to the south-west, I saw the Ngong Hills. The noble mountain rose above the surrounding flat land, all air-blue. But the four peaks looked very 25 small in the distance and different from the way they looked from the farm.

| *flush*, (of the face) to become red with a flow of blood to the skin

Questions

The Ngong Farm

1. Describe the area around Ngong Farm.
2. What are the difficulties involved in growing coffee?
3. Where did the Kikuyu live and the Masai live?
4. Why did Karen Blixen feel at home in the Somali village?
5. What kind of difficulties did white people have in understanding the natives?

A Native Child

1. What did Kamante look like when Karen Blixen first met him?
2. Explain why she was considered to be a good doctor.
3. What was the natives' attitude to western medicine and treatment?
4. How did Karen Blixen treat Kamante's disease?
5. What happened to Kamante at the Scottish Mission?
6. How was he different from the other boys?
7. What abilities did he have as a cook?
8. How was Kamante's attitude to animals different from that of other natives?
9. Describe Kamante's reaction to the big grass-fire.

The Savage in the Immigrant's House

1. Describe the natives' attitude to hard times.
2. How did Karen Blixen begin to write stories?
3. What was Kamante's first reaction to her writing?

4. How did she try to make him understand what is in a book?
5. Why didn't Kamante want to go to the French Mission on Christmas Eve?
6. What change in attitudes resulted from Kamante becoming a Christian?
7. Describe the old man, Knudsen.
8. Explain what they did when they found Knudsen's body.
9. How did Kamante and the other houseboys write to Karen Blixen after she left Africa?
10. How did she feel when she got these letters?

The Shooting Accident

1. How was Karen Blixen informed of the accident?
2. Describe what she saw when she arrived in the kitchen.
3. How seriously was Wanyangerry injured?
4. What did Karen Blixen do?
5. What did Kabero do after the shooting?
6. What did the old men come to tell Karen Blixen the next morning?

Riding in the Reserve

1. Why and how did Karen Blixen take part in keeping the peace?
2. What is the basis for justice seen through African eyes?
3. What did they imagine had happended to Kabero?

Wamai

1. Why was Karen Blixen glad to have Farah with her at the Kyama?
2. What did people want from Kaninu?
3. Describe Kaninu's relations with the Masai.
4. Exactly what happened in the kitchen on the night of the accident?
5. How did they agree that forty sheep should be paid to Jogona?
6. Why did the Kikuyu of Nyeri come?
7. What was the writer's attitude to the Nyeri people?
8. Explain why Jogona came to see her two days later.
9. How did Karen Blixen help Jogona?
10. Describe Jogona's feelings about the document and explain how it helped him.

Wanyangerri

1. Explain how the doctor at the hospital patched up Wanyangerri's face.
2. What did Farah tell Karen Blixen about Kabero?
3. What did she do after she heard the news?
4. What happened five years later?
5. Explain the change in Kabero when he came back to the farm.
6. Why did Wainaina come to the house to ask for milk?
7. Describe Kaninu's appearance when he came to see the writer.
8. Why had he agreed to give ten sheep to Wainaina?
9. Why did Karen Blixen decide to send for Kinanjui?

A Kikuyu Chief

1. Describe earlier visits made by Chief Kinanjui.
2. Describe his arrival at the house.
3. Why did the Arab merchants settle on the east coast of Africa?
4. Who helped them to conduct their business?
5. How did Karen Blixen explain Farah's attitude towards the Kikuyu?
6. What was the reaction when she explained that Kaninu should give a cow and calf to Wainaina?
7. How did Chief Kinanjui keep control of the situation?
8. Explain how the affair ended.

Big Dances

1. Where did the Ngomas take place?
2. Describe a Ngoma held in the daytime.
3. What preparations did the dancers make?
4. Explain what happened to twenty-five young men during Karen Blixen's absence and why.
5. What dramatic incident took place at a night Ngoma?
6. Why did the twelve Masai come when they knew it was against the law?
7. Who helped the injured dancers and what did he do?

The Noble Pioneer

1. Explain why Berkeley Cole was popular with the Masai.
2. Describe the Masai's reaction to the news of the war.
3. Why and how were medals given to the Masai?

Wings

1. What did Denys Finch-Hatton do in Africa?
2. How does Karen Blixen describe their relationship?
3. Give an account of how they killed the two lions.
4. What was the reaction of the children to the killing?
5. Why did Karen Blixen consider flying the greatest pleasure of her life?
6. Why did Ndwetti not understand why they wanted to go on flying?

Hard Times

1. Describe the many difficulties Karen Blixen was faced with.
2. How might she have saved the farm?
3. How did the farmers try to drive the grasshoppers off their land?
4. What damage did they do on Karen Blixen's farm?
5. What was the Natives' reaction to the writer's difficulties?

The Death of Kinanjui

1. Why had Kinanjui sent for Karen Blixen?
2. Describe the inside of his hut.
3. Why did the writer not feel that she could help the dying chief?
4. What had the Kikuyu done with the body of a dead person in the old days?
5. Give an account of Kinanjui's funeral.
6. Describe Karen Blixen's thoughts about it.

The Grave in the Hills

1. Where did Denys Finch-Hatton consider living when he could no longer stay on the farm?
2. Give an account of what happened during his last days.
3. Describe Karen Blixen's feelings in Nairobi.
4. How was the news of his death revealed to her?
5. Describe how Karen Blixen found the place in the hills where his grave should be.
6. How was Denys Finch-Hatton remembered by his brother and his old school-fellows?
7. What did the Masai report to the District Commissioner?

Farah and I Sell Out

1. How did Farah support Karen Blixen?
2. Why was it such a huge problem to find new land for the squatters?
3. Describe the writer's efforts to help them.
4. How did she feel when a solution had been reached?

Farewell

1. Why was Farah impressed by the Ngoma that the old men wanted to hold?
2. How was it stopped?
3. How did Karen Blixen feel about the old women?
4. Describe her meeting with the old woman on the path.
5. What were her feelings on the day of departure?

EASY READERS *Denmark*
ERNST KLETT SPRACHEN *Germany*
ARCOBALENO *Spain*
LIBER *Sweden*
PRACTICUM EDUCATIEF BV. *Holland*
EUROPEAN SCHOOLBOOKS PUBLISHING LTD. *UK and Eire*
ALLECTO LTD. *Estonia*
EMC CORP. *USA*

This edition has been abridged and simplified to provide
graduated reading exercises for students of English.
Vocabulary and sentence structures have been
selected because of their high frequency and practical
value to the learner.
Words which are difficult to understand in context or
fall out of the EASY READER frequency modules are
explained by footnotes in simple English or by illustrations.
EASY READERS are suitable for use in schools, for home
study, or simply for reading enjoyment. See the complete
list of titles on the inside cover.
EASY READERS are also available in German, French,
Spanish, Italian and Russian.

EASY READER TITLES NOW AVAILABLE:

Sir Arthur Conan Doyle: The Red Circle (A)
Sir Arthur Conan Doyle: The Speckled Band (A)
Lois Lowry: Number the Stars (A)
R. L. Stine: Stay Out of the Basement (A)
R. L. Stevenson: The Bottle Imp (A)
Oscar Wilde: The Canterville Ghost (A)
Oscar Wilde: The Canterville Ghost, dramatized version (A)
Enid Blyton: Five on a Treasure Island (B)
Roald Dahl: The Way up to Heaven and Other Stories (B)
Sir Arthur Conan Doyle: Black Peter - The Red-Headed League (B)
Lois Duncan: I know what you did last Summer (B)
Lois Duncan: Killing Mr. Griffin (B)
James Herriot: If Only They Could Talk (B)
Colin Higgins: Harold and Maude (B)
S.E. Hinton: The Outsiders (B)
Jerome K. Jerome: Three Men in a Boat (B)
Ira Levin: The Stepford Wives (B)
Pat Lowe: The Girl with No Name (B)
Brian Moore: Lies of Silence (B)
R. L. Stine: Fear Street: The Perfect Date (B)
Mark Twain: Tom Sawyer (B)
Oscar Wilde: The Happy Prince (B)
Richard Wright: Black Boy (B)
Karen Blixen: Out of Africa (C)
Tim Bowler: Storm Catchers (C)
Roald Dahl: Edward the Conqueror and Other Stories (C)
Charles Dickens: A Christmas Carol (C)
Sir Arthur Conan Doyle: The Hound of the Baskervilles (C)
Graham Greene: The Third Man (C)
James Heneghan: Safe House (C)
S.E. Hinton: Tex (C)
Ira Levin: Rosemary's Baby (C)
James Moloney: Gracey (C)
Celia Rees: Witch Child (C)
Mary Shelley: Frankenstein (C)
Alexander McCall Smith: Tears of the Giraffe (C)
R. L. Stevenson: Treasure Island (C)
Bram Stoker: Dracula (C)
Oscar Wilde: The Picture of Dorian Gray (C)
F. Scott Fitzgerald: The Great Gatsby (D)
Alan Sillitoe: The Loneliness of the Long Distance Runner (D)
R. L. Stevenson: Dr. Jekyll and Mr. Hyde (D)
Kurt Vonnegut: Slaughterhouse-Five (D)

ADULT:

Peter James: The Perfect Murder (B)
Stephen Speight: Doomed to Die (B)
Stephen Speight: Swindled (B)
Minette Walters: Chickenfeed (C)